ON THE JOB

A Builder's Tales

David Merron

Michael Terence
Publishing

First published in paperback by
Michael Terence Publishing in 2018
www.mtp.agency

ISBN 9781912639021

ON THE JOB

A Builder's Tales

David Merron

FOREWORD

The exposure that most people have to the Construction Industry is to its rough end – to the dodgy roofer who appears after a storm and charges gold dust for replacing a few slates, or the brickie's labourer leering at short skirts from the scaffold. And it is a rare dinner party or a pub gathering, that is complete without some tale of woe from some experience with 'The Builders'.

Construction certainly has its rough side, where mechanical excavators and concrete lorries churn up the mud, and rasp-tongued scaffolders swing from dizzy heights. With it though, comes the excitement of creating something from nothing; of turning an old bomb-site into a school or modern office-block, a neglected Victorian pile into a state-of-the-art hospital, or providing decent homes for people – and of course keeping the already-built environment in a state of good repair.

There is too the satisfaction of seeing the concrete – in the full sense of the word – results one's work and not just a pile of papers or electronic signals on a disc, though there is enough of that too in the modern construction industry. Above all, there is the sense of humour generated by confronting and overcoming obstacles – a feeling, at times, that we must only be in it just for the laughs.

Through real-life anecdote and short story, *On The Job* tells of the varied facets of the construction industry and of those employed in it, who by working together, create and maintain our built environment.

This collection also reflects a period of transformation from the 70's into the new century, when most directly employed operatives were replaced by sub-contractors and everyone in the industry had to digest the changeover from Imperial to Metric measurements, together with initiatives like Quality Assurance, Health & Safety Regulations, etc., etc. It was also a time when the industry was still full of real-life characters – names and personal details amended here – who'd left school at fifteen to learn a trade, then ducking and diving their way up the managerial ladder.

Despite the pressures and problems, at the end of each project there is a sense of achievement. In my thirty odd years of construction project management, on hospitals, museums, banks, housing, railway stations, airport and many other projects, there were hectic days, tense days and certainly, frustrating days, but I can truly say that there rarely was a boring day. Are there many other professions that provide that?

David Merron MCIOB, MSc

CONTENTS

WHO BUILT IT? 1

BET ON IT! 10

TO HADES AND BACK 21

MORE THAN THREE TIMES LUCKY 33

HOLDING IT ALL UP 43

ORANGES AND LEMONS 55

TAKES ALL TYPES 61

LEAVES ON THE LINE 73

ARS GRATIA ARTIST 87

THE SILVER SCREEN 99

ALL TANKED UP 110

KICKING THE HABIT 123

JUST A ROOKIE 133

DOING A BANK JOB 142

DOWN IN THE DEEPS....156

TRADES UNION BLUES....170

ONE TOO MANY....182

TROUBLE AT T'COUNCIL....192

BRINGING DOWN THE ROOF....205

INTERIOR BY DESIGN....215

LIFT UP....224

THE CLERK OF WORKS....233

IT'S THE CONTRACT, STUPID!....241

WHERE THE BUCK STOPS....249

WHO BUILT IT?

It was a grand, ceremonial opening. Everyone was there: the TV celebrity to cut the ribbon, the architect who designed it, the Mayor of the Borough, Portobello Residents' Association Leaders, local Radio, the press, photographers – quite a crowd. And over the following days and weeks, the new Public Conveniences in Westbourne Grove, London, with their integral flower shop that had replaced the old Portakabin, created quite a stir. They gained national design awards, glowing reports in the local and national press and full-page spreads in the specialist journals.

All wrote how it had been opened by a well-known aristocrat-cum-TV personality; complimented the architect on the concept; the local council that part-financed it and the residents' committee that fought for this original design. Mentioned in fact was everyone who had a hand in it. Everyone that is, except those who actually built it!

Amongst all the publicity, there was little more than a word or two acknowledging those who managed and co-ordinated this unusual project, and the men whose skills and labour had made it a reality. It was as if one fine day, of its own accord, thanks to some *deus ex machina,* the whole building had materialised onto the townscape from the architect's drawings.

When we were first awarded this D&B (design and build) contract for these new – and one-off-design – public toilets in West London, I wondered whether we might have our own Clochemerle epic – like the scandal in the French village that built a public toilet in the main square and created a national crisis. In the end, ours didn't quite do that, but widespread attention it certainly did attract.

The existing Portakabin public toilets, installed as a 'temporary arrangement' after the war, had after many years become permanent - and an eyesore. They had been erected over the remains of the original conveniences that were bombed in the Blitz, one of the many underground toilets that the ever sanitary-conscious Victorians, had built across London.

With their public pride, it had been provided with decorative wrought-iron stairs, beautifully tiled floors and walls, and wonderful, polished copper piping snaking in and out of the mahogany veneered cubicles. You can still see a few examples here and there in the big cities, but most have succumbed to neglect and indifference through lack of local council finance to maintain and staff them – for without an attendant they soon became haunts of drug-addicts, rough sleepers, graffiti vandals - and metal thieves.

The ruins of these original underground toilets, on a traffic island in the middle of the road in Westbourne Grove, had been partly filled in and had this temporary/permanent Portakabin plonked on top. Eventually, the council scheduled it for demolition and planned to replace with an almost equally ugly, permanent, utilitarian building.

But they had reckoned without the local residents.

With Westbourne Grove being adjacent to the well-known Portobello Antique Market, a powerful residents' committee, including many shop-owners objected to the Council's design. They organised a well-publicised and supported campaign to build something more fitting to the area, and raised the additional funds to make it happen. They also engaged a well-known architect's practice to design the new toilets as something special – as indeed it turned out to be.

When Tom, the site agent and I first saw the drawings and visited the site, we went to have a strong cup of coffee in the nearby café to recover. The new design was absolutely unique – an architect's ego trip or a brilliant concept, whichever you may choose, or both. It was shaped like the prow of a ship and built of bright green, glazed bricks, with a roof of curved, steel ribs and glazed panels, creating a gull's-wing-like structure.

'Certainly something different,' I said.

'You can say that again,' muttered Tom.

Short, smooth hair and sharp brown eyes, Tom was an experienced site agent. He had continued studying at college and was certainly bound for higher things in the Company. Which was just as well – for this project promised to require a lot of input from both of us.

Firstly, the setting-out would be a nightmare – getting the measurements of a long, irregular triangle over the rubble and void of the old Victorian toilets. It had to be precise to the millimetre to accommodate the pre-ordered, specially fired – and very expensive – green glazed bricks. These could not be cut and the quoin bricks for the corners, with exact angles, would be especially manufactured too. If our setting-out was off by even a fraction, or the corner angles were wrong by a few minutes of a degree, the bricks would not fit within the elevation lengths and the quoin bricks would stick out like a sore thumb. And with a long fabrication period, they had to be ordered at once to meet our programme.

Another urgent problem was sorting out the foundations. As this was a design-and-build contract, as yet no one had designed these and the onus was on the contractor – that was us – to get it right. This meant we had to engage the architect right at the outset, together with a structural engineer.

As the old Portakabin had been placed over the partially rubble-filled, bomb-damaged Victorian toilets, it would be like building over a large, partially-concealed hole in the ground. After much humming and hawing, the structural engineers, in their usual belt-and-braces manner, had produced a scheme of deep concrete pads and massive ground beams. The new toilets were only a single-storey building, but these could have supported the Eiffel Tower. They also would have also cost a fortune, and on a fixed-price, design-and-build contract we, the contractor, would be responsible - and would have to pay for these. Luckily, on this form of contract, we also had some control of their design.

Tom and I put our heads together and concluded that the old Victorian building must have had pretty good foundations itself – public works didn't skimp in those days. Fortunately, the local borough District Surveyor was an old-timer and thought so too. So it was concluded to dig trenches through the infill rubble down to the old floor, fill them up with mass concrete and for a tenth of the costs of the engineers' intricate design, cover the whole site with a new reinforced concrete slab.

So, we set up site and work began. Once the old Portakabin had been demolished and removed, we could take a look down. Below, partially covered by bombsite rubble, were the beautiful black, white and red mosaic floor tiles. Here and there, odd cut lengths of copper tubing snaked above the massive, white fireclay urinals and glazed tiling. Sadly it would be the last time any of this would ever see the light of day. Shortly after, the concrete lorries drew up and poured in their mix to create the mass concrete foundations. Only then could Tom accurately set out the building and the concrete foundation slab.

In the meantime, he and I had discovered that most of the architect's drawings were long on ideas, but a pretty short on detail and dimensions. This would be design-and-build with a vengeance and if we didn't take it in hand ourselves immediately, nothing was going to move.

Apart from setting out the building with millimetric accuracy and exact angles to accommodate the purpose-made glazed bricks - including a high tank-room with its glazed-brick sloping roof – all the other items, from the steel and shaped-glass, gull-wing roof, the stainless-steel doors, the vent-louvres and the interior toilet cubicles and the glass-walled flower kiosk, were bespoke one-offs. Most had to be precisely dimensioned and pre-fabricated off-site.

To ensure that once the work commenced there would be no hold-ups, the two of us, together with the architect's keen, young – and thankfully open-minded – assistant, spent hours and days in our site hut, making joint decisions and coordinating the drawings – and co-ordinating they indeed demanded. Both Tom and I enjoyed it. For once, everyone was working together instead of getting constantly contractual and passing the buck between architect and contractor as so often happens in the industry. If only all construction projects could be like that.

After we'd sorted out and modified the existing drainage and water supplies to fit the new structure, and come out of the ground, we poured the concrete foundation slab. Then Tom checked his setting-out for the umpteenth time and we began raising the walls. This work required bricklayers with talent and dedication, so we decided to engage a sub-contractor we knew well who had worked with the company on several contracts previously. Their price was higher than others – provoking arguments with our surveyors who, by nature, would always choose the cheapest one, but with the agreement of my director, he was persuaded to take them on. This was not a project for penny-pinching.

Working carefully, with humour – and the odd profanity, the bricklayers, Ed and Barry, a father and son duo - as is often the case – began making a beautiful job of the lovely glazed bricks with their neat, thin joints. They had to be 5 millimetres everywhere to meet the dimensions and the corner angles – and to persevere with this through the thousands and thousands of bricks they laid. It was like artwork.

After most of the other bespoke items had been placed on order with specialists, we had to tackle the most difficult job – the roof.

This was an arrangement of lightweight steel ribs supporting scallop-edged, glazed panels, shaped like gulls' wings. The ribs sprouted from a central steel gutter running along the middle of the triangular roof, but at the sharp end were designed to form a semi-circular fan over the glazed flower kiosk.

The specialist steel fabricators out in Essex had

produced working drawings for the steel ribs and, with our agreement, had begun fabrication. All had gone well along the two straight sections, but as soon as they came to the semicircular fan over the sharp end, the original architect's drawing for the arrangement of the ribs proved to be absolutely fanciful; they would not fit onto the designed central hub.

This part of the design and fabrication was to prove a real headache. So it was back to the drawing-board again, and after two more trips out to the fabricators in Essex together with the assistant architect, we found that the issue could only be resolved by forming different radii at two levels. So we ended up with a hub that looked fit for a Centurion tank turret – but it worked.

Meanwhile, the surrounding ground-works were well underway. The old island kerbs were taken up and re-laid to new levels with added granite kerbs – from Portugal. Holes were dug to form planting pits for 20-foot high, specified tree saplings – from Italy. One pit had to be jack-hammered out of the solid concrete remaining from the old toilets, like a gigantic flower pot. Finally the paving stones were taken up and re-laid to drain rainwater away from the building. This was another awkward job, given the building's shape and proximity to the roads either side, which of course had their own fixed levels.

Under the fan-like roof end, the flower kiosk with its plate glass walls and door was installed and married into the glazed brickwork, which was another problem solved. The young project architect had designed 'cartoon' male and female figures for the entrance doors either side, and our metal workers made a beautiful job of neatly cutting these out in sheet-steel and seamlessly fixing them to the metal doors. So now, with the building frame completed and secure, we could deal with the interior.

The toilet cubicles were re-drawn and dimensioned and sent out to pre-fabrication, all to be able to fit into the unusually shaped triangular interior. Meanwhile the electrical and water services were being installed and decorators were carrying out preparatory works.

Throughout the months we were on site, while occasionally moaning about the construction of something so unusual, all the tradesmen involved – carpenters, bricklayers, tilers, glaziers, plumbers and electricians and the other trades, rose to the occasion over and above any normal requirements, taking care to keep to the precise dimensions and adding suggestions and expertise as they went along. And finally it stood in all its green-glazed, seagull-winged glory, smack in the middle of Westbourne Grove and ready for public use.

When the day finally came to ceremonially inaugurate the toilets, I suggested getting the mayor of Kensington & Chelsea to give it a real Clochmerle send-off, and likewise raise his top hat to public cheers as he 'christened' the urinals. Alas, that was politely declined: 'No public toilet functions please, we're British!' So with press and media all assembled, the celebrity lady gave a brief speech, cut the ribbon – and it was opened.

As mentioned though, in the numerous articles and commendations that followed, everyone was mentioned, thanked and lauded – everyone that is, except those who had actually got it off the ground. And if it wasn't for the tiny, stainless-steel plaque we fixed inside the entrance, no one would know who – or if anyone at all – had ever built it!

With that kind of appreciation and recognition, how will we encourage young people to choose construction as a career, so vital to our future?

BET ON IT!

The construction industry is full of larger-than-life characters – as was Nobby, a foreman, and the success of any building contract is primarily down to the man in charge on site – the foreman, now more often called the site agent, or on large projects, site manager.

Whereas head-office staff, especially the surveyors, estimators, planners – and nowadays many contract managers – have come through college, the man on site had often started his career as a tradesman, usually carpenter or bricklayer – 'on the tools' as we say, often son following on from father. And as the paper trail grew in the construction industry - as in so many spheres of the economy - some of them struggled, but despite that succeeded.

Nobby was just such an old-timer, and we met on this contract for building Sheltered Accommodation flats in those long forgotten days when local authorities had the ambition -but also the money for social housing. As I was to discover though, for Nobby, getting the building up seemed to be a fringe activity.

Nobby owned a horse – which wasn't surprising since his main interest was in horses – the racing kind. Actually, he only owned a leg. With three other enthusiasts, he'd purchased a racehorse – a leg each, the men on site teased him.

'Still a youngster,' he would say. 'But a real winner – a cert!'

Some of the cash had apparently come from a widow he knew in Llanethly. The men reckoned he'd do better to place his bets on her rather than his nag.

The project comprised two, two-storey interconnecting blocks of flats – red brick and tiled roofs, with communal areas and landscaped gardens. It was being erected on a wedge of waste ground that had been enclosed, and somehow forgotten, when a large, low-rise, London County Council housing estate had been built in the Thirties – an estate that was to cause us much grief throughout the construction.

I had taken over the contract from a manager who had moved on to higher things in mid-contract - most probably onto a higher salary, elsewhere. He must have known for a while that he was leaving because management-wise he'd left behind quite a mess and many knots untied; the three blocks were just bare brickwork skeletons when I took over.

His departure like that was unusual. In the construction industry, with its booms and busts - often used by governments of all colours to regulate the economy, building companies are in the habit of going to the wall and new ones starting up again with monotonous regularity. 'Always keep your copybook clean', was the motto, because you never knew when you were going to meet the same people in a different configuration. The person you left clearing up the mess, might easily be the one who was interviewing you for that plum job elsewhere, a few years later.

Nobby was somewhere out on site when I drove in on my very first visit that afternoon. I had called in by chance on my way back to head office from another contract. The three blocks had reached eaves height and were surrounded by scaffolding, obviously waiting for the roof structure and the first floors were just bare joists. The site hut was empty – just a warm kettle and half-finished mug of beer-like tea - the kind that takes the glaze off the cup.

On the drawings' bench, sheets and scraps of scribbled-on papers were scattered about amongst a general melange of site-labour records and materials' ordering books. On the wall, elevation drawings of the new buildings were stuck up with masking-tape.

Searching for the rest of the drawings, I eventually found them buried beneath the spread-out pages of at least four newspapers – and in those days there were two London evening papers, as well as the national dailies. Not just any pages though – just the rear two or three of each one – on which numerous yellow streaks highlighted that day's racing selections

As I lifted the corners to glance at the drawings, Nobby burst in.

'Hi,' he puffed, nodding. 'Heard you were comin' my way. You beat me to it!'

As usual, the foremen's bush-telegraph had been buzzing. On this informal network, news travelled round the sites faster than you'd get an e-mail through these days. Even office gossip – who was leaving, who had been promoted, or who was knocking-off with whose secretary. True or false, everything would be common knowledge on site long before we knew at head office.

Nobby was nearly six feet tall, with a long, sharp face and large hands that moved continually as he spoke - and a heavy smoker, a cigarette butt usually dangling from his lower lip.

'Just a mo', he gasped, plonking himself down at his

desk, 'jus' gotta make a few urgent phone calls.' Thinking it was to chase up last minute deliveries of materials or to bawl out some sub-contractor who hadn't turned up, I turned back to the drawings' table and casually raised the racing pages again to look at the drawings.

'Hang on,' Nobby called over. 'I'll sort 'em out for you in a minute.' I stepped away from the drawings; site foremen are usually as possessive about their own patch as any proud housewife. He then plunged into a serious conversation over the phone. Material deliveries? Subcontractors? No chance.

'Have to get a bit of advice,' he grinned, hand over the mouthpiece as he listened; then he put down the phone and dialled again

'Hello. Fred. Yes. Two thirty. Chepstow,' he continued, reeling out a number of names. 'Yes, treble up. No. Not that nag. No. Rovers Run. Sure. A cert.' A questioning voice seemed to come through the ear-piece, but Nobby just shook his head. 'No. It's a cert. Got it hot, just a minute ago.' It was just two o'clock.

He slammed down the phone, stood up, held out his hand and we shook. 'Nice to meet you,' he nodded. 'About time the office gave me some back up, I can tell you.' He picked up his mug, then turned. 'Want a cup of tea?' Seeing the state of the table, I said I'd just had one.

'So,' I asked as he took a few sips of his, 'how's it going?'

'Going like a rocket,' he smiled. 'Running at Newmarket on Thursday. In with a good chance the trainer says.' I tensed – then paused for a moment. Take it easy. It's our first meeting. Need to make contact first.

'Good luck,' I said, and after a pause as I glanced

through the window, added, 'So how's the job going?' trying not to sound like a repeat questioning.

'Oh. That? That'll be okay. Got it well in hand.'

I could feel that he was dying to sort out the three o'clock and the three thirty, but with what must have been a supreme effort, he shrugged and crossed over to the table. Carefully he folded back the newspapers, laid his hand on the drawings and pulled out a vertical section.

'Roof.' he muttered. 'Bloody architect and engineer couldn't sort themselves out with the fixings to the brickwork.'

The roof structure was a composite arrangement of steel trusses that the engineer had designed to take the weight of heavy, concrete roof tiles, and a complex arrangement of timber rafters and struts to make up the roof hips and valleys that the architect had drawn.

'Anyway,' he continued, 'I told them what we were doing and they agreed. Doin' their bloody job for them as usual.' Whatever I thought of Nobby's pastime – or rather his almost full-time – pursuit, through long experience he'd learned to duck and dive to resolve site problems. 'Lucky we got a good foreman chippy on site,' he added. 'Chris has got the roof timbers sussed too.'

Chris, it turned out, was a carpentry sub-contractor. He worked with a small band of men, and for a little extra had agreed to supervise the erection of the roof structure. I subsequently learned from Nobby that Chris had it real tough, his wife having disappeared with another man about six months previously and leaving him with three children. Luckily, they were all of school age and even luckier for him that he lived locally. So he needed the site as much as we needed him.

Chris managed to give his kids breakfast then take them to school, before arriving on the site each day. Then he would nip off again at four to take them round to a friendly neighbour and return to work until five thirty, to make up the time. He did this every day and sometimes came in on Saturday morning to sort out a tricky piece of preparation for Monday morning for when his whole gang turned up.

The man must have had an iron constitution to have stood up to the stress. He was already lean and wiry, but every week he looked leaner and more haggard. I sometimes wonder how he managed after the contract had finished. Probably became a misogynist for life.

It was fortunate that we had Chris, for as the work progressed I suspected that had we relied on Nobby alone, the trusses might still be on the ground. I had further doubts when we came to the finishes. There was a lot of specialised fitting-out for the old people and although Nobby was certainly au-fait with the main structures, I wondered whether he was up to sorting out the internal finishes.

The contract was about two thirds through however, and even if I had wanted to, there was no way we could replace a foreman without a load of disruption. In addition, it would also give the architect a way out at a later date, should there be a dispute about delays. I shouldn't have worried. Nobby applied himself to the job in his own ducking-and-diving way, and the project continued to progress well.

It being one of my first contracts with this company, I decided to spend more than usual time at the site –

which was just as well because telephone communication was a problem. I should have realised this immediately but somehow didn't twig when the day following our first meeting, I phoned in the afternoon to enquire whether the new roof tiles had arrived. The architect had changed the specification and the new ones were on long delivery.

Nobby's phone was engaged. I tried again a few minutes later and it was still engaged – and so on for about an hour. Suddenly I remembered the back pages of the evening papers. Nobby was obviously on the phone to his tipster or his bookie. After that, I never bothered to phone him after lunch. No wonder the surveyor had pushed the last quarter's site telephone bill across to my desk with a big red question mark on it.

Nobby's long experience of ducking and diving also had other advantages. A gang of kids from that neighbouring Council estate persistently plagued us, little monsters of between eight and twelve years old. As it was a large site with a new perimeter road, extensive landscaping and new drainage, we could only erect hoardings around the actual buildings. Even so, every morning when Nobby opened up the site, something had been damaged: windows broken, fence pulled down, a stack of bricks scattered or timber strewn across the mud.

One night the kids untied the lashings of a painters' cradle, and sent it hurtling down to the ground below; it would have killed whoever might have been beneath. Their favourite trick however was to lift up the heavy, cast-iron, road-gulley gratings and drop them down the gulley pots, some of which were two or three feet deep. God knows how the little blighters managed it – the gratings weighed over a hundredweight each. Some mornings, two men had to spend a couple of hours re-setting them.

One Thursday a week or two later, when I collected Nobby's weekly sheets and petty cash vouchers, there was an item for "site expenses", three pounds fifty, unspecified.

'What's that for?' I queried, knowing that my surveyor would ask me the same question.

'Blood money,' grunted Nobby.

He'd caught hold of the gang leader, a lad of about twelve and related the resulting exchange blow by blow:

'"Here," I says to their ringleader. "You're in charge of this lot aren't you?" 'Course the boy denies it, but I seen it all before – many times,' grinned Nobby. '"Listen," I says, looking the boy straight in the eye, "see this fifty-pee bit?" The boy nods. "Well, it's yours each morning those gulley tops are all in place. Okay?" The kid nods again if bribery and corruption's the normal thing. "An' if there's any gratings down them pots," I says, "even one. Nothing. Savvy!" And the boy nods again. Not a blinking word all the time. "Right," I says, "so here's the first fifty pence. And don't spend it all at once." An' the little bugger just nods, takes it and strolls off. Probably spends it all on fags,' he muttered. It was before kids had moved on to heavier stuff.

Blood money or not, the gratings stayed put until we tarmac-surfaced the road and handed over. I sometimes wonder onto what that lad progressed afterwards. Probably doing time as I write.

Well, the roof trusses were hoisted, erected and

secured and the roofs tiled, and once all was watertight, sanitary ware and electrics were installed and decorations were taking place. So all was proceeding well, when on Derby Day I happened to make an early site visit. It was morning tea break and the men were gathered in the canteen hut. Spread out amidst the sandwiches and mugs of tea on the tables were the daily papers, back pages uppermost; Nobby was taking bets to place with his bookie, advising or pouring scorn on this choice or that.

'Here, Dave,' he called over, as I walked in. 'What's your fancy?'

'Not a betting man,' I excused myself, not wanting to be drawn into gambling on site.

'Go on,' he pressed. 'Have few nicker each way. What can you lose? Here,' he smiled with largesse, 'I'll put it on for you.'

'No. Not really, Nobby.' Then I hesitated – not wanting to seem a killjoy either. So, thinking fast and looking for a way out, I pulled a pound note from my wallet: 'Tell you what. I'll choose a name, Nobby. You lay the bet. And share any winnings with the boys.'

'Well take your pick,' said Nobby, 'but you're missin' a good chance to make a few bob!'

I shrugged and ran my finger down the list of runners on one of the back pages.

'Black Knight,' I said finally.

Nobby grew apoplectic.

'That nag,' he scoffed. 'Won't even get to the first corner. Don't wanna waste good money on that!'

I shrugged.

'My choice, you said. I just like the name.' And as everyone laughed, he hurried out to phone his bookie while I went to drive back to the office, thinking no more about it.

The next day I had to come over early to sort out our agenda for the architect's fortnightly site meeting later that day. As I crossed to the site hut, I noticed two of the men leaning over the scaffold rails, grinning.

'What's up,' I asked Bill, one of the brickies.

'Here,' called back, 'just wait till you see Nobby. He's choked!' He was.

'Lucky bugger, you,' Nobby grunted as I walked in. 'Your's came in at fifty to one. Sure you don't want it. You'd be fifty nicker up?'

I shrugged and smiled.

'No, like I said. Divide it between the lads.' Then in an afterthought added, 'what about yours, Nobby?'

'Bloody useless.' He scowled. 'Shan't ask him again. Do it on me own from now on.' Not that he seemed to have more luck that way either, judging by the fact he so rarely crowed over any winnings.

By the autumn the job had progressed almost to conclusion. New paint gleamed from the window frames and front doors, turf had been laid and grass was sprouting anew on the lawns, and the council was painting yellow lines on the fresh tarmac. Each day, eager young social-workers appeared with old people in tow, checking out their new flats. And Nobby's newspapers continued to cover the drawings' table – right to the bitter end.

Now, taking the mickey and a good wind-up is part

and parcel of building site humour, never malicious, but taxing sometimes all the same. And Nobby came in for a full measure of it from the men on site, regarding his poor choice of winners. Even more, they teased him about his horse. But just a week before the handing-over ceremony, Chris caught hold of me as I drove in one day.

'Take it easy,' he murmured. 'Nobby's real gutted.' Then glancing both ways added, 'his horse has broken a leg.'

'Which one, Nobby? Yours?' they'd all been sorely tempted to joke, but knowing how cut up he would be, had kept shtum. As I entered the site hut, he looked up, eyes half closed and nodded but didn't mention it. Neither did I.

Well, when the job was successfully signed off, Nobby left the company and went down to Wales. I never saw him again. The men were right. He would have done better to have placed his bets on that widow in Llanethly. And he must have done just that.

TO HADES AND BACK

Every building project, however similar to one you have just completed, presents a unique set of problems to be solved, which is what makes construction management so stimulating. It certainly makes it stressful at times. But boring – never! So when our company landed a contract to construct a large, new Church Community Centre over a medieval graveyard, I knew there was certainly not going to be any chance of that.

This Church Centre project had floated off the architect's drawing board during the Eighties. It was a period when the ecclesiastical authorities were going into community work in a big way. Realising that only the deeply pious would want to sit in a gloomy mediaeval building when there was East Enders or Coronation Street on TV, they began to sponsor the creation of friendly social centres and child nurseries, with bright rooms, kitchens, carpets and coffee corner.

Many churches owned properties or parcels of land from mediaeval village days. These were now in town centres and thus extremely valuable and sought-after, commercial sites. Selling them off would provide the necessary finance for the new buildings.

On this project, Fred, the Site Agent was an old-timer foreman and ex-bricklayer, short and almost as wide, with mop of short, greying hair. There were not many things about the game that he hadn't met before. But for him too, this project was a first. And the completely unforeseen and hair-raising event at the start of the contract was also unique – for both of us.

The churchyard hadn't been used for over a century

and had recently been de-consecrated – no simple matter in itself. First, the diocese had to agree, then publish notices of its intention. Anyone wanting to remove headstones or graves was given six weeks in which to do so. In addition the Home Office had to grant a licence – and that required eight weeks, with announcements in the press, and so on. Sometimes the two ran together, but either way it was a long process and even if the architects had a scheme in hand, only then could things start moving.

As often appears the case, by the time the contract was signed, we had to commence ground-works and foundation trenches just as the clocks went back and the weather was closing in. This was common to so many of my projects and seemed to be result of a process that must go something like this:

Come Spring, the developer's or client's thoughts turn to an idea for a project. Through the summer the architect works on the scheme and presents it – but that is just when the client/developer jets off to their long summer holiday in the Bahamas or similar.

On their return in September, they realise that everything has stood still, so there is a frantic rush to prepare and cost the contract and send it out to several contractors for competitive tender and receive back the quotes. Around October a contract is signed and a start date agreed. And so just as the days shorten, the rains fall and winter is approaching fast – ground works commence. And this contract, despite its specific aspects, was no different in that respect.

First, all the headstones had to be carefully taken up and removed. Day after day, under the huge trees already shedding their leaves, our JCB excavator trundled across the site, carefully carrying half a dozen removed stones on its front bucket, to be neatly re-erected around the perimeter wall. Finally, just when the ground looked clear, we discovered a number of lozenge-shaped, horizontal gravestones hidden in the long grass, probably medieval. The local archaeologists had a field-day, which further delayed the work.

Having got through all that, Fred reckoned that considering all the problems, the excavations, and concrete foundations and ground slab were going really well. Until that morning.

Now, as he waited for someone at the other end to pick up the phone, Fred was sitting on the edge of his chair in the site office, mumbling to himself.

'It's God punishin' me, so help me,' he was thinking as he picked up the telephone again, convinced that he was paying penance for the way he'd behaved earlier that morning. 'Len was right,' he muttered as he dialled again, 'shouldn't have been so short with that poor woman.'

Gripping the receiver, he stared through the hut window. Thirty yards away, lying on its side like a wounded beast and with its rear end trapped in a gaping hole, was a huge, laden, concrete lorry. Twenty-five tons of steel and concrete – and the concrete slowly setting solid inside the drum.

The earpiece clicked and he barked into the mouthpiece again. A crane was supposed to have arrived but hadn't. Yes, it was on its way, the voice at the other end assured him.

'Before Christmas!' he snapped and slammed down the receiver. Yes, if it hadn't been for them bloody vaults, Fred was thinking.

On the site plan, the architect had shown the location of all the known underground vaults. In the data box in the bottom right-hand corner however, was a warning note: 'The contractor is responsible for checking that there are no further unmarked vaults that may interfere with the works' – the invariable get-out clause.

Fred reckoned he had checked as far as he could and had set out the site road to avoid them. Fifteen truck-loads of concrete had been brought along the same track across the graveyard without mishap. Now the damn sixteenth had gone just a foot or two to the right of all the others – and found one. Yes. Must be God punishing him for being so bloody callous, like Len, had said. Too bloody right.

It had all begun earlier that morning. While the men were in the hut having their tea break Len, a brickie, tall, fair-haired and ruddy-faced, noticed two people walking around the churned-up site, a well-dressed man and a woman. He pointed it out to Fred.

Fred ran out.

'Excuse me. Excuse me,' he shouted over. 'Can I help you?'

Gingerly treading through the mud and hardcore, the two came across to the hut. She was dressed in a long brown coat and matching hat, he wore a smart jacket and wide-checked trousers. American, thought Fred. They were.

'We are just over on vacation,' said the woman,

looking puzzled, 'and thought we might find my great-great-grandfather's grave.'

'Well, this is a building site now,' said Fred. 'It's closed to the public, I'm afraid. Insurance liability and all that.' Then, as an afterthought, he added, 'Any idea where it was?'

'Somewhere over there,' she said, holding up the sheet of paper she'd been looking at while anxiously glancing across the site. 'Near the tower end of the church, my cousin reckoned.' Fred followed her gaze. A thick concrete ground slab now covered that area.

'Well I tell you one thing, missus,' he chuckled, 'come Judgement Day he ain't never goin' to get up. That's for sure!'

The woman didn't seem to share the joke. Dropping her hand, she took the man's arm and, head down, turned away. Quickly they walked back to the road, the man turning to cast a short, sharp glance at Fred as they went.

'You're a heartless bastard,' said Len, as Fred came back into the hut. 'She was right upset, she was.'

'Well, it's not as though the old bloke popped his clogs yesterday,' huffed Fred. 'Americans! No sense of humour!' And now, three hours later, that truck had hit an unmarked vault.

Fred sighed and leaned on his desk. Nothing to do now except wait and hope. If the concrete went off solid in the drum, it would be better to dig a damn great hole and bury the lot. No ordinary crane could get anywhere near enough in the churned-up soil to lift that load safely. And just his luck, now when they'd got over all the other problems in the ground they'd encountered.

Most people imagine a village churchyard as a serene place of rest, where ancient bones lie untroubled through the centuries. In fact, for the same half-acre to embrace all the deceased over hundreds of years, in most churchyards the entire area had been turned over again and again, previous occupants being pushed aside to make room for the next century's dead or new ones buried on top. Which apparently is why many churchyards are much higher than the surrounding area.

As part of our signed contract, we had to collect up any bones uncovered and have them reburied to the vicar's instructions. Well, we'd reckoned on cutting through a few graves with the foundation trenches, but the reality was something quite different. The whole area was full of them.

Throughout the work, as each grave was uncovered in excavating the trenches, the bones were carefully dug out and put into plastic sacks. Usually, however, there were three and sometimes four skeletons, one on top of another, often down to eight feet deep. We had no idea there could be so many.

Gerry, the curly-haired ganger, had a macabre sense of humour. He'd line up the skulls along the trench top, and as they would sit grinning at him in the half-light of a winter's afternoon, he would point along the row.

'B'Jeasus. Just look at them teeth on that one,' he would quip. 'Bite your head off on one go.'

At the end of each day's work, the sacks of bones were taken to one of the larger vaults remaining and deposited there, with the vicar saying a prayer or two. This particular vicar was very keen to have the church centre completed – said he was more concerned with the living than the old bones underfoot. 'The souls have long departed anyway,' he smiled as we chatted over the logistics of working amongst the graves.

Well, Fred had got over all that. The groundworks and foundations had been completed and he'd poured most of the concrete ground slab. Now the walls were beginning to rise – heavy, brick cavity-walls faced with knapped flint and supporting new, prefabricated stone-capped buttresses, all to match the old church.

Bricklayer gangs were often a family affair and Fred's son, also a brickie and Len, soon became skilled at fitting the knapped flints onto the brick walls. Fred reckoned that given a hundred years and bit of modern pollution, they would match in nicely to the old church fabric.

Obtaining the knapped flint had not been simple. Once upon a time they were waste from local chalk quarries. Now only one or two people supplied them, dredging the flint nodules at low tide off the Kent coast where they had fallen from the famous white cliffs, and splitting them apart. Attempts to use local, round flint-cobbles somewhere up north had proved highly dangerous. In hard frosts, trapped water had expanded, shooting them out of the walls like miniature cannon balls...

Now, as Fred sat staring through the hut window, he was cursing his luck. This had been the last concrete lorry of the day. Yes, the last damn one needed to finish off the main entrance slab. And it had found that unmarked vault – a deep one at that.

Again, he pictured the whole episode – the lorry backing slowly, the drum turning and young Billy, the apprentice, signalling it to come on. Suddenly, a horrible cracking sound and the offside rear wheel slowly disappearing into the ground up to its axle, then another crack as the vault walls must have crumbled completely. After that, as if in a slow-motion film, the whole rear of the truck sinking in up to the churning drum before, and just as slowly, keeling over.

Fortunately, when the driver had felt the first lurch, he'd slammed on the brakes and jumped out of the cab. Running round to the rear, he'd stood with the rest of the men, horrified and helpless as the truck settled, rolled on its side. The drum, caught fast in the mud, must have stalled the engine. It cut out, leaving a deathly silence as it came to rest. Then everyone began shouting what to do – before realising they could do nothing, while the driver held his hands to his head moaning, 'Oh my Gawd. Oh my Gawd.' Most of the drivers were self-employed and were paid so much for each delivery by the concrete company. This was his own truck.

'Who's gonna pay for this lot?' he shouted as Fred charged out from the hut.

'Never mind about the bloody money,' snapped Fred. 'Gotta get the concrete out before it sets hard.'

He set the men to work, scooping it out with shovels and buckets, but they could only get a foot or so inside the rear hopper.

'The cleaning hatch,' shouted the driver. 'Get a spanner and open the hatch.' At the front end of the drum was a man-sized plate used for occasional cleaning out of the drum. Tim, the carpenter, raided his toolbox and soon had it off. Some of the concrete did flow out and down into the vault, after which the men extracted as much as they could. It was like Pooh Bear scraping honey out of a pot, smiled Joe, the plumber, who'd been reading it to his kids each evening.

Fred had already phoned the head office. I happened to be on another site at the time and received an urgent phone call telling me what had occurred. Immediately, I started phoning around, trying to organise a large mobile crane. By pure chance, one plant-hire company just half an hour away from the church had a crane being serviced in one of their yards.

'Forget the service,' I called down the phone. 'This is an emergency,' and jumped into my car. When I arrived on site the men had done as much as they could and all work had stopped. Everyone was standing by and looking on, helpless. And there was still about eight tons of concrete left inside the drum – setting fast.

'The crane is on its way,' I said, trying to sound encouraging.

'Crane'll never lift this lot,' the driver was whining. 'And what about my ruddy truck?'

Suddenly Fred had an idea.

'Fire brigade,' he shouted. 'The fire brigade is just up the road. Let's get 'em to wash it out!'

A frantic phone call and my promise of a very meaningful contribution to their Christmas Fund brought the huge red engine up to the site entrance. And as though it was a real blaze, the firemen smartly rigged up a long hose and with a roar from their engine, a strong jet of water shot into the drum.

A weak, water-concrete slurry began surging out of the hatch and from the rear hopper, all pouring down into the vault - which seemed bottomless and swallowed whatever came out. After about half an hour, there was just some shingle and water left inside the machine. We'd saved the drum and taken out a lot of weight, but the rear of the truck was still securely anchored in the gaping vault.

A short while later, the crane arrived, prompting delicate negotiations.

'Not backing onto that lot,' grunted the driver, viewing the chaos. 'When I put my jacks down there may be another bloody vault.' The prospect of a twenty-ton crane stuck in the ground as well as the lorry made us stop and think. But somehow we had to get that truck out of the vault.

'I'll sign responsibility,' I pleaded, 'and we'll check the ground as you come back,'

The negotiations took a good quarter of an hour, and eventually he was persuaded to back into the site. But after only a few yards, he jumped out and looked at the ground, and again the arguments began. We knew that without him getting closer to the truck, there was no chance of lifting it. So with Gerry and Tim crawling along in front of the crane and stabbing the ground with bits of steel reinforcement as if clearing a minefield, inch-by-inch it crawled back about ten yards and again the driver stopped and came round to see for himself. He looked at the gaping, shattered vault roof and the black hole beneath, then shivered; a few yards away on the far side of the hole, were two of Gerry's grinning skulls.

'That's as far as I'm comin',' he croaked turning a pale shade of green, before hurrying round to the hydraulic controls.

With the engine roaring, the huge offside-rear jack slid out. Slowly, like some space module settling on the Moon, it settled onto two old railway sleepers Len had prepared. The sleepers creaked and sunk halfway into the ground. The leg extended further, putting the whole rear weight of the crane on that one leg. We waited, holding our breath to see if the sleeper and the soil would hold up. If they took all that weight, then the ground would surely take even the combined weight of the truck and the crane when all the jacks were lowered.

Grudgingly, the crane driver lowered the other jacks on sleepers, took a good look underneath the crane, then agreed to try. The men fastened slings around the rear of the truck and as we stood and watched, and tried to look knowledgeable, the driver like some prima-donna on centre stage, took control of the hydraulics again.

The engine roared, the slings took the weight and with the concrete-truck driver eyeing his machine and thinking of his profits rapidly ebbing away, inch by inch, like some latter-day Lazarus, the stricken machine began to rise up from the tomb. As soon as the chassis was clear of the ground, Gerry and the others quickly slid more sleepers underneath to take the weight, the slings were re-fixed and to everyone's relief, the whole of the rear was swung up and clear, then gently lowered down upright onto its own wheels.

As the men wrapped up the slings, the lorry driver climbed up into the cab and sat for a few seconds. Disconsolate and still in a state of shock, half-heartedly, he played with the gear lever and controls then happened to turn the ignition key. Amazingly, the diesel engine sparked into life. A few minutes later, the astonished man engaged gear and very slowly drove out to the hard-stand by the site gateway. There, the truck stood as if nothing had happened, with only black mud on the rear chassis and a dented door to show that it had been halfway down to the underworld and back. In relief, we cheered – firemen and all – and with his first smile of the day, Fred signed the sheets.

The truck, the crane and the fire engine soon drove away, and the men went back to work. As we walked towards the hut, Fred suddenly stopped and glanced up at the sky. I knew that he was thinking of what might have been, if… if the fire brigade hadn't been so helpful, if the crane hadn't been in a local depot getting its service check, if the driver hadn't jumped clear, or if any of the men had been working in a nearby trench. He turned to me and shrugged.

'Well, considerin' everything,' he said, 'I suppose Him up there wasn't as nasty as he could have been.'

At that moment Len walked past.

'Teach you to be a bit more considerate next time someone else comes looking for an old grave,' he grinned - he'd already told me about the incident with the woman. Fred winced, we all laughed.

He went into the hut to write his report, and I drove away to the office to squeeze that cheque for the fire-brigade fund out of my project surveyor. That would be almost as difficult as extricating the truck.

MORE THAN THREE TIMES LUCKY

It was late on Christmas Eve and eerily silent. For a moment I couldn't believe that I was standing in the middle of one of the world's largest international airports. No planes landing or taking off, no luggage trolley-trains on the move, no baggage handlers scurrying about – and absolutely no passengers.

A cold, Easterly wind was blowing across the bare, concrete apron as I walked out of the rear cargo doors and left the Heathrow terminal building to check on the progress of our contract work. Out on the silent runway, beyond the glare of the yellow floodlights, large ice-white patches glowed with a strange iridescence – yet we'd had no snow at all. Curious, I walked towards the nearest one. Suddenly a ripple spread across the surface and the whole patch seemed to float sideways. It wasn't snow or ice, but a flock of white-plumaged seagulls roosting for the night, they too taking advantage of the stillness, huddled together against the cold and all facing the same way into the wind.

The sound of hammering shook me out of my trance. I turned back and walked towards the terminal building, reflecting that even with the best planning, you still need the odd stroke of luck. And in this awkward contract, without several of them, it could have been disastrous.

In the Eighties, with the rapid growth in air travel, Heathrow Airport had decided to completely reorganise its passenger baggage-transfer between its then three terminals and the waiting aircraft. As a temporary handling facility, we had to design and construct three large loading-platforms, one for each terminal. The problem for them was however, that this was a 24/7 working airport. No way could they allow builders onto the working areas.

So the management decided that all three terminals would shut down completely on Christmas Eve, and we were given a 36-hour window of work to complete the contract. By the morning of Boxing Day all had to be complete. And since we were working on the aircraft side of the terminals, there could be no ifs and buts or maybes about that.

Christmas Eve! Who on earth would want to work from Christmas Eve, were my first thoughts on being handed the contract at head office. It would require much more than financial inducement to get steel fabricators and carpenters to work on those two days. I needed someone who owed me one and would do it as a favour. Eventually I managed to locate them and began twisting arms, together with offering 'financial inducements' - a nice Xmas present, to compensate for the inconvenience.

Having found those willing and able to give up Christmas with their families, there was the small matter of security clearance. And there is no way anyone can work on the aircraft side of an airport without that.

These were in the days of IRA activities England - the Bishopsgate bomb and others. Only a few months previously a mortar bomb had been fired into the airport from a perimeter road, so everyone concerned was on high alert. And as I was to find in my later contracts in Whitehall, with the preponderance of Irish names in the building industry, I knew it would take a while to get that clearance for some of the men designated to work there.

With only four weeks to organise and programme the work, I had waited anxiously as each day passed without the clearances coming through, wondering who I would approach if this or that sub-contractor's men were refused clearance. In the event, most were cleared in time. My first stroke of luck.

As in many public institutions where we worked: museums, railway stations, theatres, etc., once you pass through from the public to the working side, you enter another world. So it was behind the scenes with the airport.

Baggage handling is an integral part of air travel. When we go on holiday, as our luggage disappears onto that black conveyor belt behind the check-in desks, we take it for granted that bar a few, well-publicised incidents, our cases will all arrive at the same airport as we do, and on the same plane.

At the time, everyone's luggage came spewing out onto a low ramp. Here, the handlers identified it by the tag-strip fixed at the check-in desk then loaded it onto miniature railway trains of trolleys tugged by a small tractor, to be taken around to the appropriate aircraft. So as I stood at the rear of Terminal Two planning how to organise our work, while watching the baggage men handling hundreds of cases, I was amazed not by the fact that there might be the occasional case going to the wrong aircraft, but that practically all of them *do* get onto the right one.

The new system designed by the airport, involved replacing these trolley-trains by a fleet of small, automatic-geared trucks to speed up things, but they needed these new, large platforms to coordinate the loading.

In order to work out delivery routes for our building materials and plant, a few weeks previously I had obtained permission to drive onto the aircraft parking aprons. Here, you rub shoulders with the myriad workers and machines that you only catch a glimpse of as you wait in the departure lounge or by the boarding gates, and who keep the whole shebang going.

Rolling along just a few feet from my car were the ten-ton, aircraft towing-tugs, looking like huge, steel packing-cases on massive rubber wheels. At top speed they travel at just a few miles an hour, but with that weight are unable to suddenly stop. If you inadvertently veered into their path, they would leave you flattened as surely as if you'd been run over by a steamroller.

Driving to the rear of Terminal Three, I suddenly found myself cruising under the droopy nose of Concorde. Even a glancing brush with that single front wheel would probably have landed me in the Tower. Little wonder that our company had had to take out a special, multi-million-pound insurance policy to be allowed to proceed with this contract.

The new loading platforms had to allow for rapid demounting and removal in the future, when a more advanced system, still at planning stage, was ready. So they were to be fabricated in lightweight steel sections, with plywood decking covered by hard-wearing, maple-strip flooring. Lightweight and demountable they may have had to be, but with thousands of cases being thumped on them each day at an international airport, there could be nothing temporary about their actual construction.

In an amazingly short time, our steel-fabricator's engineer worked out the design, which we submitted to the airport's chief surveyor. He had no objections and fabrication commenced. Apart from ensuring the future, rapid-demountable bit, it was a simple construction of welded, angle-iron frames, bolted together in sections. And to save time on site, instead of drilling and screwing the timber boarding to the steelwork, we proposed to shot-fire steel pins through the plywood decking into the steelwork, before secret-nailing the maple-wood, strip flooring – no nail-heads protruding to snag the cases.

The airport had agreed to our delivering the steel frame sections, plywood and boarding the day before Xmas Eve, and all was ready for the off when suddenly we had a phone call from the Airport surveyors. It appeared that as well as the overall management, each terminal had its own supervising engineer and the man from Terminal 3 didn't think the plywood boarding was sufficiently rigid for the purpose – despite the additional maple flooring. In vain we protested that the design had been approved by the airport management! He said he personally wasn't satisfied that three-quarter inch ply was man enough and – he warned – even if we erected it, he wouldn't authorise its use for his terminal.

It was panic stations all round. The work was due to begin the following evening, the materials were on site – and we were responsible for the design as well. I had visions of cases left strewn all over the tarmac around Terminal 3 when the post-Christmas rush began. We needed a miracle – or some good luck.

Phoning up our fabricator's structural engineer at his

home, he reluctantly abandoned arranging his Xmas tree and faxed over calculations to show that the 3/4" ply would indeed take the loads specified – just, he said.

'And that's with your usual 500 percent safety coefficient,' I joked. 'So it must be okay.'

'Had to reduce it down to just 200 percent just for you,' he laughed. Either way, I knew that the original steel fabricator's calculations had been sufficient. Catching our own engineer at home and not on his way to a sunny Christmas holiday was my second stroke of luck.

That same day I drove to deliver the calculations personally to the obstreperous terminal engineer's office – only to discover that as he would be working over Christmas, he had the day off. Having dug in his heels though, he was certain to pay us a visit. Panic stations again. I couldn't risk his slapping a veto on us and condemning the work. Decisions, decisions.

'Well, let him eat cake,' I said to Brian, my surveyor. 'To hell with the expense. There's too much at stake.' We would have to use the thicker plywood he demanded. But how on earth would we get it in time? Everyone was closing shop for Xmas Eve.

Frantic telephone calls around the London timber merchants found one who was still working - just before they closed at midday. A financial inducement to their delivery-men brought a special delivery of the meatier 1-inch plywood for the Terminal 3 platform. That was my third stroke of luck.

I already had the pre-ordered guns, pins and cartridges in my car, but the thicker plywood would now require longer nails – which in turn would need stronger shot-cartridges and heavier gun and it was now midday!

I jumped in the car, and made a mad dash up the A4 to the hire plant depot at Southall, collected the new shots and nails and a more powerful nail-gun and drove back. So, at last everything was ready for the off.

Since the short-haul flights using Terminal 1 had finished early for Christmas Eve, to assist us, the airport allowed us to start work there at two o'clock in the afternoon and we got going. The steel fabricators set up the first frames and the chippies immediately began to cut and fix the ply decking. Since the designated loading areas in the terminals were not at all square, there was quite a lot of time-consuming, cutting-in on the ply decking to fit the spaces between the existing concrete piers.

To avoid any hold-ups, we had tried out all three nail-guns on the first frames, including the heavier gun I'd brought for the 1-inch ply. But as luck would have it, at about four o'clock that first afternoon, that one heavy gun packed up. Just wouldn't fire! The hire company manager swore they had tried them all out the day before in their yard when I picked it up, but as usual Murphy's Law was operating –'if something can possibly go wrong – it will.'

Well, to complete the works on time, we couldn't do without the heavier gun. Panic stations again. It was now late afternoon on Christmas Eve. Everyone in the plant-hire depot must surely have gone home by now.

This was before the days of the now ubiquitous small mobile telephone. Luckily, Ron, the carpenter sub-contractor had one those new, heavy car-phones that required charging every day and a Land Rover to carry them around. Using that, without much hope, I phoned the plant-hire office. Amazingly, the secretary was still there and answered the phone; my fourth stroke of luck - the workers are always the last to leave. But the manager was out, she said and everything was locked up. My heart began to sink. But after I explained the situation, she promised to try and contact him. Could I phone again in ten minutes? I guessed he'd probably gone too and I'd just get a home phone number, which would be useless. He lived way out in the sticks.

The minutes ticked past. I phoned again. The secretary was still there. Yes, the manager had indeed finished for the day, but by pure chance was having a Christmas drink with mates in a nearby hostelry before going home. She had phoned him there and explained the urgency and he had promised to phone me. Promises, promises, I was thinking but a few minutes later he did phone from the pub saying I was lucky to catch him, but he couldn't drive out to us – he'd had, you know, etc., and a friend was giving him a lift home. But if I could come and call him out from the pub, the plant store was nearby and he'd accompany me to open it up and find me a new gun.

The A4 was busy of course; everyone seemed to be going somewhere for Christmas Eve. As I drove East, the last, long-haul planes were coming in to land. It was a strange sensation watching a string of landing lights shining in the sky, starting faintly from somewhere over Docklands and growing lower and lower and brighter and brighter as one after the other the aircraft came towards me, their beams pointing towards the runway. I shuddered to think what would happen when the long-haul 'planes started coming in again on Boxing Day and the Terminal 3 platform wasn't ready.

It was dark by the time I reached the pub.

Reluctantly tearing himself away from the bar, the plant manager came across with me, opened up the stores and took out a new, wrapped, heavy-duty gun and gave it to me with extra shots and nails.

'This one's fine,' he said, shooting a pin into a nearby timber baulk.

'So was the other one, you promised,' I moaned.

'Look.' He shrugged. 'I'm giving you a brand new one. Just arrived from the manufacturers. You're lucky. All the others are out and we keep it as a spare.' That was my next stroke of luck.

I drove back to the airport and handed over the new gun. To my joy, the first platform at Terminal 3 was already taking shape nicely. We'd previously warned the airport authorities to inform their staff that there would be shot firing. Still, given the tense security situation, I wondered how many of their staff took cover when the first shots rang out!

Finally, with all the men co-operating and conscious of the tight programme, in four, twelve-hour shifts, over the two days we just about finished on time, and managed to clear everything away and tidy up, just as the airport was waking up again and the first planes started coming in on Boxing Day.

A week later, I drove back to check on a number of minor snagging items. Around the front of each platform we'd fixed a heavy timber and rubber buffer. The previous ones on the old loading docks had been in a sorry state. By the way the new trucks were backing into them, these probably wouldn't be in a much better condition shortly.

On our new platforms, cases were being thumped about and piled up, often several high, but they took it all without a creak or moan. I wanted to go and bring the Terminal 3 engineer to see and for him to come and eat humble pie. His one-inch ply boarding at short notice hadn't come cheap. But I decided to let it ride. After all, when you get not just one, but so many strokes of good luck on one contract, there's no point in knocking it.

And I still have nightmares of what could have happened without any one of them.

HOLDING IT ALL UP

Underpinning – creating new, solid foundations under buildings in danger of collapse – may be one of the less glamorous projects in the builder's world, but it is a vital one, and illustrates many of the problems faced and overcome in construction work.

Unlike much of modern building work, generally this operation cannot be mechanised and relies on the skill and muscle-power of those involved, and as such is often undervalued - as the following anecdote might illustrate.

We had a contract to build another Church Social Centre, also in the churchyard of a medieval church. Unfortunately, cracks had appeared in the south wall of the old church tower, adjacent to where the new centre's foundations would be. A trial pit revealed that a void had developed under the old rubble foundations and threatened the tower with serious collapse. We had already set out the new building and were geared up to start, but before we could commence the main contract, our first task now would be to underpin and secure the old tower.

When we held the first, fortnightly site meeting, it was a freezing day, a light fall of snow had covered the ground and leafless trees stood out, black and gaunt against the grey sky. By chance, during the meeting in the site hut the architect happened to comment at 'just how much money ordinary labourers were getting these days!'

After the meeting, as we passed by the tower on the way to his car, crouching in a deep, frozen, muddy trench, two men were urgently excavating a pit under the foundations of the medieval tower in preparation to pour in concrete and stabilise it.

Nodding to the mud-spattered men as one scooped a heavy spadeful of wet clay out onto the frozen, white grass, I asked him pointedly:

'Well, how much do you think that job is worth?'

I don't remember his answer – I think it was something like an embarrassed grunt...

Subsidence. It was those long hot summers that created the problems. Some time in the late Seventies they were, the years – and the temperatures.

Much of London and the Thames Valley are built on clay, and with our usual English weather most of the time clay is damp and stable. Until those balmy summers. Day after day, a scorching sun baked water out from the soil, while nearby trees often added to the catastrophe by sucking out the last available moisture.

Clay, as it dries out, begins to shrink. And if the hot weather is prolonged, it continues to shrink, leaving empty spaces under foundations. Since the drying out is rarely even, some sections of the foundations will sink more than others – Differential Settlement, we call it. Houses that for a century or more have stood as though on solid rock began to show cracks in their brick walls, as different sections of their foundations subsided.

That particular summer, as the cracks in walls grew wider – and in some cases you could slip a hand through them, insurance companies were deluged with subsidence claims. But as in so many instances, one person's grief can be another's joy – in this case, the builders'.

To ensure that the affected wall didn't fall down or that the house wouldn't develop a severe list to starboard, someone has to dig down and expose the void underneath, then fill it with concrete to secure the foundations. And once the foundations have been secured, there is brickwork to repair, cracks to be made good and everything to be plastered and redecorated. In short, underpinning is inevitably an unwelcome, expensive building project.

Subsidence had always been around, the most severe cases being over shallow workings in the old coalfields. And there were always specialist companies that dealt with underpinning either in this way, or with specialist equipment. In the late Seventies however, the floodgates opened. Anyone who could wield a pick and shovel, and trundle a wheelbarrow became 'an underpinning contractor'. The builders had never had it so good. It was as though some divine force had copied the idea of providing employment to glaziers by paying little boys to break windows.

Although there are patent methods of securing sinking foundations that rely on specialist equipment and expertise, the most common method is as explained above: to manually dig below the existing foundations to expose firm ground, then to create new concrete foundations. Since such excavation leaves the existing foundations hanging in the air, so to speak, the work can only be done in a piecemeal fashion.

In practice, a length of foundation is divided roughly into metre sections and only one in every three or four is dug out at a time. An added complication is that most houses are neither isolated, nor in the middle of a field;

invariably they are in terraces or semi-detached, or adjacent to other buildings. And all have drains, cables, gas and water mains - often unmarked, as well as gardens and paved areas around them.

In addition, especially in older houses, some internal walls have their own foundations, and in prolonged droughts the drying out extends right under the building, so those walls can subside too. It then becomes a case of removing furniture and floor coverings, and taking up floorboards etc., even before any underpinning can begin – as in the case of one smart, detached house in Harrow with which we had to deal.

On my first visit with the architect and his structural engineer, it wasn't the house that so concerned me, but the surroundings. On every side were intricate brick patios and steps, as well as landscaped gardens with mature bushes. With the entire perimeter of the house due to be underpinned, a brief survey told me that the surrounding area would soon look like a bombsite. In addition, the foundation of an internal concrete pier that supported part of the roof had also subsided, and would have to be underpinned too.

As we sat with the architect and his client, a gentle, diminutive widow, in her immaculate lounge with its designer soft furnishings and timber panelling, I just hoped he had informed her of what was coming.

This was a problem builders often face: the architect or surveyor being 'economical with the truth', in order not to jeopardise receiving the commission. So when informing the owner that their house had to be underpinned, little is ever mentioned about the actual work involved, and it is left to the contractor to gently covey the full horror story - and to mollify the owner once work had commenced.

On this contract, the house was in a small, tree-lined cul-de-sac, along with half a dozen equally expensive houses. Did the neighbours know what could be about to hit them?

Anyway, before we began, everything was carefully photographed and recorded, inside and out.

'Got to look like this when we've finished,' I said to George, the site agent when we surveyed the site. George was an old-timer - greying, black hair and sharp brown eyes. Knowing how sensitive we had to be with the lovely house, I had asked head office to release him specifically for this project.

'Hope our estimator at the office has priced for all of that,' he muttered when he arrived and looked around. Whether he had or whether he hadn't – and my waters told me he hadn't – that was how it would have to be when we finished.

At the start, we engaged a professional gardener to carefully remove most of the shrubs. Some he left in the ground.

'Won't survive replanting,' he winced. 'Pity.' And I hoped the architect told the lady that as well.

Well, the occupier moved out and we moved in. Up came the lovely pavings and steps, all stacked on boards on the lawns, while trying to avoid damaging the remaining plants. Then we divided the foundations' perimeter into metre sections – there were about forty of them – and with two gangs of men we tackled about six sections at a time, digging pits a metre deep alongside the foundations for access.

At each separate section, a further metre depth had to be dug out underneath the foundation itself, to remove the desiccated clay and create a void in which to place our concrete. So as we dug these pits down and under the foundations, huge mounds of soil began to appear everywhere. Soon, the whole area began to look like Flanders 1917, while earth spilled across the garden and against the neighbouring fences and hedges.

Out of courtesy, we'd informed the immediate neighbours of the works, but they, like the client, had no idea of what was coming. Soon anxious phone calls reached me at head office, demanding to know what was happening. When I explained, the silence at the other end seemed to indicate their wondering whether the dreaded plague would hit them too.

With the first three sections dug out and ready, in came the structural engineer. He had to agree that the soil that we'd exposed, often a metre-and-a-half down, had not dried out either and was sufficiently firm. In this case, the man was a very experienced old timer – the type of engineer it's a pleasure to work with.

The young ones just out of college or part of a large practice, go back to their textbooks and then apply a 500 percent safety coefficient, so that you end up doing ten times the amount of work actually required. The experienced engineer takes out an old envelope, scribbles a few figures, then after satisfying himself of the situation - and that we have done something similar many times before, fixes the next inspection and leaves us to it.

This particular engineer was so much an old timer that he came with a walking stick – which didn't prevent his climbing down the ladder into the trench. Then, taking his stick, he stuck the point into the clay and put his weight on it.

'That'll do' he said as the point stuck in less than half an inch. And after a few more probes along the trench, he pronounced the subsoil suitable and climbed out, heaving and puffing, but under his own steam. 'Be back on Wednesday for the next lot,' he said and went on his way. Casual it may have seemed but nothing escaped him. On further inspections, in several places - especially near the drains, he found soft spots and we had to excavate another half a metre down. This entailed shoring up the trench with timbers and creating a massive pit under the foundations – but firm ground underneath it had to be.

Next, we shuttered up and poured concrete into these pits. Unfortunately, as it sets concrete shrinks slightly, so this would have left an air-gap under the old foundations and they could have slipped again. To prevent this, a two-inch space is deliberately left between the top of the concrete and the underside of the foundations, which, the following day, is packed up with cement mortar, rammed in tight. After allowing another day or two for the mortar and concrete to harden off, the access pit is backfilled with soil before adjacent holes are dug out and the whole process begun again in sequence. Of course the concrete now takes up space that was once filled with earth, and this spoil has to be barrowed out and taken away to landfill.

With the perimeter being secured, we then had to approach underpinning the internal pier – in the middle of this beautifully furnished lounge. First, we employed professional carpet-layers to carefully take up and store the carpets, then specialist joiners, to remove adjacent built-in cupboards and panelling. Steel beams were bolted to the pier and the ends supported on props and boards to take the weight of the roof. Only then could we dig out the dried up clay under its concrete pad and form new foundation as before.

Meanwhile, slowly and in strict sequence, we progressed around most of the entire house. At the end, it had massive concrete foundations on which you could have stood Canary Wharf Tower. But there was no alternative if subsidence was not to happen again in a future dry summer – and of course to satisfy the insurance company who were paying the bill. Many insurers took a massive hit from the multitude of claims that year and upped their premiums accordingly.

With concreting and backfilling completed, it took several days to remove all the excess soil from site with much arduous manual work, barrowing it out to the cul-de-sac to be picked up and taken away by grab lorries. The reinstatement also took several weeks - re-laying the paved terraces and paths, bringing back the gardener to restore the garden as best he could, and then engaging the specialist joiners and furnishers to deal with the interior.

During these works, we were glad that the lady had booked into a hotel some distance away and didn't see the organised chaos all around the house. When she came back, we were just sweeping up the pavings and paths and the gardener was planting the last of the replacement shrubs, so apart from the odd smear of clay here and there and the new shrubs, to her great relief – and ours – it looked much as she had left it.

We shook hands with her and her son, who had come with her and drove away, thankful that she hadn't seen the chaos a few weeks previously.

In another underpinning contract at red-brick, Victorian house in Hampstead where everything is on some slope or another, as well as at one wall and corner, the drying out subsidence and slippage had also affected some internal supporting walls, including a huge chimney-breast. The problem here was that this very room had gorgeous parquet flooring with the wooden blocks bedded on pitch, so they could not be taken up without damage.

By chance, there was a metre-high void beneath the floor. So in order to preserve the parquet, we suggested going beneath through an adjacent room, and work like miners beneath the floor to underpin the chimney-breast. Of course this would be an expensive operation, but after much to-ing and fro-ing between the owner, the surveyor and the insurance company, the latter agreed the extra costs. Replacing that beautiful parquet flooring would have cost them much more.

Once we had dug out the first trench, there was sufficient room for a man to kneel or crouch in the workspace, which made it slightly easier, but the process was prolonged and laborious – shovelling and wheel-barrowing the clay out, and then bringing the concrete in from the mixer-lorry on the road outside.

While this was going on, we had to underpin one the walls at one corner of the house that was threatening to slide all the way down into the Finchley Road. Because of the slope, it required massive new concrete foundations, which again could only be carried out piecemeal, so the whole contract took several months.

When we had finished, repaired, redecorated and reinstated the earthwork slope and lawn, apart from the new mortar joints in the stitched, brickwork cracks no one would ever guess that so much of the house had been underpinned.

A few years later, one day as I was passing that house by chance, I noticed that it had a Blue Plaque fixed high up on the redbrick wall, right near that underpinned corner. It announced that Beatrice and Sidney Webb, the famous socialist, economists and reformers, had once lived there, adding to my satisfaction of having saved it from collapse.

Sometimes, dealing with subsidence – or the threat of it – was less onerous.

We were called to a large, detached Thirties house in a leafy suburb during the following summer. One corner of the house had begun to show severe cracks down the brickwork – evidence of subsidence under the foundations.

The client's surveyor suspected that the drying out had been aggravated by a huge tree in the adjacent garden. It was quite close to the house and since only that side of the house had been affected, we agreed with him that its roots were obviously drawing out all the remaining moisture from the clay soil beneath the foundations. It seemed therefore, that there was no point in dealing with the subsidence without removing the root cause – an appropriate term in this case.

In vain the householder tried to negotiate with the neighbours to remove the tree, warning that it would do the same to their own house in time. Nothing. I suppose sometimes one gets neighbours like that. They could have gone to court and sued, but chose the wiser course of letting the builders deal with it rather than the lawyers – quicker and cheaper - and without Latin.

So all along the rear garden party fence, opposite the corner of the house, we dug a long, narrow trench about eight feet deep. Then we cut off all the invading roots, some of which were inches thick. Then we inserted galvanised, corrugated-iron sheets along one side and poured in concrete to within a foot of the top of the trench. And after backfilling the trench with topsoil, we laid down a strip of turfs.

With that completed we repaired the cracks in the walls of the house by stitching – which is cutting out the split bricks, inserting new brickwork and then raking out and re-pointing all the affected joints.

When I inspected the property a few months later, I couldn't even see where the trench had been. But of course, any roots trying to come through from the neighbour's tree would have received a bloody nose.

While we were carrying out the work, the man next door was observing us from an upstairs window. He looked the type who would have relished a lengthy court case. We weren't sorry to disappoint him.

And so, to return to the architect and the men down that frozen trench at the church, with which our story began. Well, the massive, mediaeval church tower wall was over four feet thick, flint-faced and filled with rubble, on rubble foundations. So it became more like surgery; excavating just sufficient space beneath one short length with trenching spades and trowels, down to firm ground, then temporarily propping up a section of the foundation to avoid more collapse, before pouring in a new concrete foundation and packing it with cement mortar as usual.

Since the exposed, medieval rubble foundations could collapse or be washed away in a sudden thaw or downpour, there was no way we could halt the work for bad weather. Hence those 'miners' crouching in that sub-zero trench.

No, it wasn't brain surgery. For those men it was just another case of underpinning. But they were dedicated to do the job and took pride when it was complete, in the knowledge that the old church tower had been made safe and sound for another few hundred years.

Underpinning became a regular part of our work, but it never returned in such quantity again as during in those years. Neither have the summers – though with global warming, it could easily do so one day.

ORANGES AND LEMONS

'...I owe you five farthings,
Say the bells of St. Martins...'

St Martins in the Fields Church in Trafalgar Square, is known all over the world from the famous nursery rhyme, its portal and tower on every tourist brochure of London. So when we were handed a contract to construct a new cafe and restaurant in the old crypt, I knew that not only would this be a one off, but that all eyes would be turned on us to make sure nothing went wrong in the process.

A medieval church had probably stood there when there were indeed fields, with its own churchyard, but by the early18th century when the new church had been built, engulfed in the growth of London there was no room for a churchyard. So huge, cool crypt had been required under the new church to house the parish dead on hallowed ground. (Evidently the bodies of the King and Queen of Hawaii, who succumbed to measles while on a state visit, once lay there, prior to shipping back home!).

By the 20th Century, the crypt was no longer used and had become just a huge, empty, dark void and when I first went to look at the site, as the surveyor took me down a flight of dismal steps into the crypt, I was surprised to see such a huge, open area down below the famous church. Rows of thick, stone piers supporting brickwork arches, marched away into the darkness in both directions, the feeble electric lighting making it look quite eerie - the perfect backdrop to a Hammer Horror

Film.

While preserving the church's main religious function, St Martin's, like many other ecclesiastical authorities, was branching out into social and commercial enterprises to enhance its income to help maintain the old structure, as well as to support its various activities – holy and secular. Creating a smart, underground coffee-bar and restaurant in this popular tourist area would be an integral part of their project. And daunting and creepy as the old crypt looked, our job would be to make it just that.

We held a joint site meeting with the architect and church authorities in one of their offices adjacent to the church to discuss procedure - and of course the need to avoid any damage and limit any inconvenience to their many activities. Having built new community centres in several churches prior to this, none of this was new to us, but of course at such a prestigious site, it had to be even more so.

The crypt had been emptied of all the old lead coffins and any other remains, but it was still an eerie sensation to sit in the dim interior between the huge pillars and arches as we discussed our work programme. Apart from the intended restaurant in the crypt, running off from the main area were a number of underground vaults and passages which also had to be enhanced - but more of those later. Meanwhile, above ground we were allotted part of an area at the rear of the church inside its ornate railings, destined later to become an arts and craft market, in which to set up our site huts.

My site agent, Harry, was a burly ex-paratrooper and had started his career on the tools, as a bricklayer. With our having worked together on several contracts –

including one in the middle of Piccadilly, I knew this awkward and prestigious contract was in good hands.

Our first task was to set up better lighting so that we could see what we were doing, and meanwhile my surveyor was sorting out sub-contractors – whose major problem would be to find parking places for their vehicles and to unload materials in this congested area. Equally, it would be a problem for our lorries to take away waste material and rubble in the heavy traffic around Trafalgar Square. And our only access at the time was the one flight of steep stairs leading out to the pavement in Ducannon Street.

Well we set up site and our first task was to carefully lift-up long rows of the slabs for the electricians to lay cable trunking for their services all around the hall and for the heating engineers to run their pipes to the serving counters area and wall heaters. The crypt had been built to remain cold – and cold it was - until we had installed some space heaters for the men working there.

The church had already removed all the lead coffins and any old bones – or so we thought, until in lifting some of the pavings we came across a few bones. These were put into plastic sacks and handed to the church authorities for reinterrement. Some of the paving stones were in fact 18th century gravestones so a delicate touch was required during this operation to avoid any damage. (At one side of the restaurant, those we re-layed can still be seen).

After the electrical and mechanical services had finished carcassing, we had to go over the whole area, stone by stone to level out the floor, repair damage and remove any trip hazards. Then it was cleaned and sealed, and it was time to move upwards.

Given their age, the huge, square stone piers and arched brickwork above were in quite good condition but of course they had to be made good, odd bricks replaced to match, and any open brick joints filled with new mortar to match - a delicate job - before it was all professionally cleaned and sealed by a specialist company. Then the electricians could install the new uplighters high on the piers, which by illuminating the brickwork arches, would provide a lovely soft light throughout the restaurant.

There was much work in the adjacent lobbies to the crypt, repairing brickwork and floors, making new openings, and plastering and tiling and decorating the walls and flooring. These areas became modern kitchens, store rooms, and new toilet facilities, transforming dismal, grubby passages into state of the art public services.

Once this was all ready, in came the catering equipment company to set up the kitchens and install the long, stainless steel serving counters in the main restaurant.

Running off from the main crypt, were a series of parallel, long arched vaults which probably also once held lead coffins, and had been used as shelters during the war. Some had been taken over by the Chinese Community in London as a social centre, and others by the church for temporary sleeping accommodation for local homeless. These areas were also dismal and grubby, so in parallel with our main contract, it was decided to refurbish them too.

This required not only flooring and decorations, but

new electric lighting and heating but more importantly, better ventilation. So we installed long lengths of metal trunking, strapped up to the roofs of the vaults, with convoluted ducting running out to new ventilation fans in the courtyard above as, well as heating services. When we had finished and handed over, it was gratifying to see these original dismal spaces transformed into bright and welcoming, social services' units.

While all this was going on, works were proceeding above ground. Behind the railings in Adelaide Street, we took up and re-laid the pavings then erected a line of stalls' spaces with ornate cast iron piers and beams, and electric lighting, into which various arts and crafts people could set-up stalls, turning this whole disused area into a colourful marketplace.

Our final and probably the most delicate task, was to take down and remove the old bells.

Having been ringing 'five farthings' for over three centuries, some of the famous bells were worn and one was even cracked. Engineers also suspected that the constant ringing had vibrated the stone and brickwork of the famous church tower, causing structural cracks. So it had been decided that they had to be removed. Fortunately, the church had found an eager buyer for the famous bells somewhere in the USA, but first they had to come down.

The deepest bell was very weighty, so the problem was how to bring them down to ground level in the confined space of the bell tower and inside the church safely and without damage to the bells or structure. It was time to call in the specialists.

First, they securely bolted a powerful electric winch to

the stone floor of the bell-tower and ran high tensile cables up to the bells' loft, where further shackles and pulleys were fixed to safe anchorages. Then one by one, the bells were attached to cables and released from their fixings, for the winch to slowly lower them to ground floor. I still have a photograph of them sitting on the church floor, waiting collection and transport to Southampton and the ship across the Atlantic.

Well, nine months later, we handed over the completed restaurant and service areas, dismantled our site set-up and left site - and the restaurant opened its doors. A few years later, as it gained in popularity, a new, larger entrance with circular stairs and lift was cut into the north courtyard for easier access.

It was the kind of contract that makes construction so rewarding, and whenever friends from abroad come to London, I can't resist taking them there for coffee or a meal, while admiring the original brickwork arches and re-laid, stone floor, still looking good and doing their excellent jobs after three centuries.

TAKES ALL TYPES

The construction industry with its macho image - as well as work for unskilled men on weekly pay packets and no questions asked, has always attracted its fair share of villains. Gary was a bit of one too – a principled one, but a villain for all that. He was also a man of many parts, amongst other things: roofer, welder and scrap-dealer. And as someone who would sort any awkward jobs, he was a valuable contact.

Garry had a past – and of course a present. But he kept that side of his activities well away from of our work and we didn't probe. Now and again though, his 'extra-curricular' ways would surface, as when one of our directors found that his newly ordered BMW was held up at the showrooms.

'Here, Gary,' he said, catching him with me in the plant-yard one day, 'you've got connections in the motor trade, haven't you?'

'Depends,' he smiled. 'What are you after?'

'Well I've got a problem with my new BMW. It's ready for delivery but they can't release it because it hasn't any windscreen wipers. And they're held up through a strike at the factory in Germany. Can you pick up a pair of wipers for me somewhere?'

Gary thought for a moment,

'BMW. Window wipers you said?' His eyes lit up. 'No problem, squire.' He leaned forward and dropped is voice. 'Look. I'm going down Bournemouth the weekend. Bound to be one or two new motors along the sea front. I can easy pick a pair off of one of 'em one night for you.'

The director's face blanched white.

'No, no. No need,' he said hastily. 'Thanks anyway, Gary. I think I'd better wait.'

'Suit yourself,' shrugged Gary. 'You're in for a long wait though.' And strolled out to the next job.

Gary had been a boy soldier in the days when parents sent their troublesome teenagers into the army 'to learn 'em a bit o' discipline'. The army readily accepted them and many were taught a mechanical trade that stood them in good stead later on. Gary had learned sheet metal working but they hadn't done much for his general education, leaving him pretty illiterate and a bit of a rough diamond. So back in civilian life, he'd learned to live off his metal-working skills – and his wits: welding, collecting scrap, used cars and then dealing in odd bits of real estate property, legally - and various other kinds of portable property – less so. Still, that was his business and we never enquired.

With an old mate of his – and I mean old – he worked for us on small-scale demolitions and metalwork, as well as pitched-roofing, so he was invaluable on our maintenance contracts. If there was an awkward job that others didn't want to tackle, Gary would get stuck in and sort it out. And on his feedback, we'd write up the specification and costs so that he – and we – could get full recompense for it.

For this Local Authority contract work though, he had to itemise his invoices – no lump sums on scraps of paper, or cash-in-hand-and-no-questions-asked. So after every few completed jobs, I would invite him into my office and together we would sit down and sort out the wording and detail his costs, all of which gave him more of a return, for which he was eternally grateful, and of course it helped us too.

In the meantime he continued with his own affairs on the side, but was very careful never to mix the two, and we developed a really amicable working relationship that later developed into a kind of friendship.

During work time, in his baggy trousers and torn grey shirt, hair all over the place and dirty smudges on his cheeks, Gary often looked as though he'd been dragged backwards through a chimney. At weekends or when he went out to his club though, it was a complete transfiguration: razor-creased black trousers, white shirt and gold chains and rings – his old truck left in the yard and his Merc highly polished. As far as we knew he'd never had married, but he was forever doing up a kitchen or a roof, or some other odd job for – or with – this lady or that.

He sometimes regaled us with tales of his trench warfare with the Income Tax Inspector, into which he would rope in his accountant. He seemed to owe twice as much to the Inland Revenue, as I would earn in a year.

After one hearing, he told me this story a few days later.

'Well they questioned me why I had so few invoices an' that, an' lack of "other documentary evidence" to support my claims. So I puts on me best cockney-cum-ignorant accent to tell how I couldn't keep track of them and "just puts everyfin' in a cardboard box, like."'

Evidently, his accountant played along, backing him up with: 'and as you can see sir, my client is not a very well educated man. Quite unused to these complicated tax matters.' So when someone else might have landed in gaol, Gary got away with staged payments over three years.

Not that villains are specific to the building industry. It's a toss-up between us, and the used-car business, and he maintained that the police force attracted its fair share too – 'takes one to know one', said Gary. Mostly however, he and other building villains managed to maintain the boundaries, keeping their extra-curricular activities at a distance. Occasionally though, the villainy did surface on site.

We had this contract to remove and rebuild the complete outer skin of brickwork from a twelve-storey, concrete tower block along a main road in North London. This '60's boom years' building had flexed and moved with time and tempest. So poor workmanship and insufficient wall ties had allowed some of the face brickwork to become detached from the concrete core.

As a result, the odd brick had already worked loose and fallen onto the pavement below, so there was an increasing danger of their delivering severe headaches to passers-by. So we were contracted to remove the entire outer brick skin, floor by floor, then bolt in heavy angle-iron supports and completely re-build a new brickwork skin with epoxy set–in wall-ties, all twelve stories of it - and with the building still in occupation.

The demolition was an awkward job requiring careful planning and phasing of removing the old brick skin to allow carpenters to fix the angle irons, on which the brickies could then build the new brickwork. It had to be carried out floor-by-floor, starting from the top floor and working downwards, all in sequence while keeping all the other trades gainfully employed – and the tenants mollified. It also created a huge amount of rubble, all of which had to be hauled along the scaffold lifts and then tipped down a chute, with all the accompanying noise and dust – again trying not to annoy the tenants and neighbours too much.

By the very nature of the work, demolition gangs are usually rough diamonds. This particular gang my surveyor had engaged though, were the tops – or the pits – whichever you prefer. At least half of them had indeed done time and were quite open about it. At the time, two were awaiting sentence for an 'affray' (or GBH as it is known in the trade), outside an East End pub. The boss himself surely had form – though what for we weren't certain.

So when the gang didn't turn up one Monday morning, Harry, my foreman let it ride. But when they missed out on the Tuesday as well, things were looking serious, threatening to hold up the other trades and knock back our programme. In a fractious phone conversation, their boss snapped that they were losing money and wouldn't come back ''till it got sorted!' but agreed to meet me on site the following morning.

He and half of his gang were already on site when I arrived just before 8.00, and arguing amongst themselves – sounded like over wages. I had to get to a meeting at a different site that morning and didn't want to hang about. Without thinking, I walked over and tried to call the boss away – and found myself looking into a face flushed with anger and a finger wagging about two millimetres from my nose.

'Listen. I've had it up to 'ere with you lot!' he snarled. Afterwards, I consoled myself that it could easily have been a clenched fist. Harry, my ex-paratrooper, burly site agent was already on his way over, but stopped a short distance away, waiting, as the man suddenly seemed to regain control. Then turning to his men, he shouted to them to 'get up on the f---n' scaffold or he'd sort them out too!' Thankfully, when he turned back, his hand was by his side – and I started to breathe again.

It appeared that he was indeed making a loss on the job and had only part paid his men – which is why they didn't turn up. Unfortunately he did have a genuine grievance against the company. My surveyor, anxious about the possibility of the crew pulling off, was holding back more of his money in retention, than usual. An explosive compound.

Eventually, I managed to calm him down and keep his men on site by promising to release what he was owed. Yes. It was a financial risk but I didn't want Harry or myself - or both of us ending up at the local A & E department, or the site-huts torched. And I was sure they were perfectly capable of all that – and more.

So I arranged for him to meet my surveyor urgently at the office later that afternoon to release their full stage-payment. Somehow that morning's confrontation must have been a catharsis, for from then we had no more trouble. And many months later, this awkward contract finished on time and made its mark-up.

I suppose the archetypal dark-horse characters at one time, were the scaffolders – though that may now have changed by now – the jack-the-lads, many of whom were said to be in and out of 'stir' between spells on the job. Although they are considered to be the rough end of the industry, I never ceased admiring the way they could balance on one pole fifty feet up in the air to tighten couplings' bolts or pass a board up to the next high level. Or the way they would weave their way through cars and people with thirteen-foot poles on their shoulders, without a scratch to either. Loading, unloading, hoisting and assembling the hundreds of scaffold tubes, couplings and boards for a huge frontage scaffold is no joke either, and requires good planning, expertise – and a lot of hard graft.

Conscious of this, I rarely argued with the scaffolders themselves on site. If they were cutting corners with the diagonal bracing or throwing and bouncing couplings off the pavements to endanger the public, I would be on to their manager to sort it out – which inevitable he did by putting a few f----s into them. And strangely enough, the managers or bosses themselves often seemed to be amongst the most even tempered in the trade, softly spoken and with serious hobbies like professional Karate, promoting youth club work, charities and so on, yet able to come on heavy whenever their rough-end charges threatened to get out of hand on site.

On occasion though, in opportunist mode, I had to take advantage of our villains' skills.

On one Central London contract, when the men turned up for work one morning, despite the prominent notice on the gate, some anti-social neighbour had parked his 4-wheel Landrover drive right across our site entrance. Concrete lorries had been ordered the day before and would already be on their way. We began to panic.

The boys tried 'bumping' it but the car was in gear as well as hand-braked, and wouldn't move. So we knocked on all the adjacent houses, many of which contained a dozen flats, and as it was in Chelsea, no doubt giving many their first early waking for quite a while. No one admitted ownership and the situation was becoming desperate. I envisaged a queue of concrete lorries churning away all down the Kings Road, unable to discharge their loads and drivers threatening God knows what.

George, the bricklayer gang foreman on that job took me aside.

'Listen,' he murmured, 'I can get it moved if you want.'

'How?' I asked.

'Never you mind,' he said, and glancing up and down the road added: 'Look, Dave. You just go for a walk. Don't want to get you involved.'

'No damage!' I cautioned.

'Don't worry,' he nodded.

So I made myself scarce for about fifteen minutes – with a cup of strong coffee at a nearby cafe. When I returned, the car was about twenty yards down the road. The boys had joyfully parked it on a double yellow line, 'teach the bugger a lesson,' smiled George.

'Great stuff,' I said. 'But I don't want to know.' Then couldn't resist adding, 'but anyway, how did you do it?'

George looked around furtively then reached into his jacket pocket and produced a ring of what must have been around a hundred car keys.

'Been collecting these since I was a nipper,' he grinned. 'Always come in useful.'

Like I said: I didn't want to know more.

Real trouble came not from any of the real villains, but more from the apparently 'straight', petty thieves –

usually temporary site labourers. When there was a good price for scrap metal, from time to time, rolls of lead would disappear from site stores and even from the workplace itself. It wasn't the value of the stuff that mattered so much as that it often disappeared at a crucial moment and craftsmen were held up waiting for replacement, losing valuable time and money. The thief probably got a pittance for the lead or ironmongery and it was heavy or awkward to take away, but still they would take it.

More serious were thefts of electric tools, especially Kango hammers and drills, often from a secure site, evidence that it was 'an inside job', though we couldn't prove it. Not that the thief made much money. He would fence it to someone who dealt in stolen tools, ground off the index number and sold it on in a distant part of the country. But it was the pettiness that so angered us. More serious was that it created a climate of suspicion that affected morale on site, not knowing who it was and perhaps fingering the wrong person, since nothing could be proved.

Because of the growing number of these tools' thefts, each worth several hundred pounds or more, builders' insurance companies raised the excess on site tools to a thousand pounds, so there was usually no redress. Finally we, like most contractors, installed heavy steel, lock-up chests in which it was obligatory to lock up all 'walkable' tools and materials every night. But still, the opportunists managed to make off now and again with the odd drill or pair of bath taps.

Whenever we lost plant or tools from site, they were rarely recovered. A whole network of villains existed, 'recycling' stolen plant around the country and even shipping more valuable stuff abroad in containers – like the three large mobile generators stolen recently and discovered in an old dockside warehouse, awaiting shipment overseas.

There was also the odd humorous incident.

We were converting a listed Victorian hotel, which had those very high, ornamental ceilings. So for internal high-level access, we'd purchased some lightweight towers, which could always come in handy on future contracts as well. The problem was that they came in even lighter-weight sections, great for handling and assembling but also very easy for 'walking' after hours. So thinking it would make then more secure I had them patch-painted with the company's yellow and blue colours.

As they were drying out in the yard, Ken walked past, glanced at me and stopped dead, smiling. Ken was the ganger of groundworks' subcontractors who had worked with us on several contracts.

'Very pretty,' he muttered. 'What's that all for?'

'Well, ruddy thieves will think twice now before taking them, won't they?' I said. 'The police will easily identify them if they're stolen.'

Ken gave me that knowing look, touched the side of his nose.'

'Not really,' and smiled. 'When they want to sell them on to some dodgy merchant, they'll just say "got a bit of paint on 'em, mate, okay?" And the bloke will just knock a few quid off.' After that we chained them up every night.

Villains like Gary though had their own code of conduct and were as sickened as we were by the petty thieving from working sites. 'I'd hang 'em up by their b--ls,' he would say. And although Gary was always straight with us, the company he kept after work did concern me at times.

One day after I had related a sorry tale of the costs to my wife's car repairs, he took me aside.

'Sounds like you got a real duff motor there,' he muttered.

'Well, we bought it second-hand a while back.'

'So, why don't you just get it 'written-off', so the insurance will pay for a replacement?'

'Can't. Just like that. And she's certainly not looking for an accident!'

'Look,' he explained, 's'easy. Just park it in a country lane near a pub one night. I'll let you know where. I know a bloke, an' for fifty nicker he'll torch it for you. Make it look like kids just took it for a joy ride.'

'I'll have a chat with the wife,' I said, feeling a bit like the director and his windscreen wipers. 'Let you know.' We never discussed cars again.

When I changed jobs and moved from his area, Gary and I parted company, though we did keep contact with the occasional fish and chip meal at weekends. And from time to time, he would appear with presents of perfume or small luxury items for my wife. We didn't ask from what lorry they'd fallen off, or where they came from – and he didn't say.

'Wouldn't involve you in any real crooked stuff,' he said, 'all straight,' then smiling, adding, 'well, maybe just a little bit curved, like.'

Eventually, I moved on and we lost contact. A rough diamond – with a heart of gold.

LEAVES ON THE LINE

There was a time when little boys all wanted to be engine drivers. With the demise of steam and the rise of the computer though, those dreams have certainly changed, but for my generation with a residue of that romantic attachment, the allure of working on the railways will always be there.

Once you enter railway property 'backstage', you become aware of a distinct culture – as well as a specific array of risks and hazards never previously encountered. Even having worked in construction which, apart from the coal mines, has amongst the highest accident rates of all industries, you have to acknowledge the potential in railway work to double or triple those figures. Very soon you become acutely aware of the specific hazards and imbibe the many strict regulations that have developed over a century and more, to avoid them.

Working alongside the track, you can be within a few feet of a train thundering past at 120 miles an hour. Inside a terminus, a train gliding into the buffers just on its own momentum is so silent, that you could easily be run over if you happened to be on the same track looking the wrong way - which nearly happened to a gang of our electricians while stretching cable-trunking along the side of a platform at Kings Cross!

With much of the network electrified, you are also never very far from 20,000 volts AC overhead threatening instant demise, so no one is allowed to work within 9 metres of the cables. A carelessly raised scaffold pole or length of steel-trunking would prove fatal. And in the 'third rail' electric systems running on 650 volts DC, a careless step and your foot would be held fast while the current would fatally fibrillate your heart in no time.

So all this was a completely new field for us when we took on a multi-million pound contract to install structural fire protection and escape measures, and sophisticated alarm and emergency lighting systems for the newly privatised Railtrack, in all the mainline London stations.

Without delay, we had to familiarise ourselves with the specific terms and language of the track – called the Permanent Way or P-Way, in which there is the four-foot, the six-foot, the ten-foot and the Cess.

The four foot gets its name from the pair of rails on which the train runs, which are the traditional 4ft.81/2 inches apart – a dimension that arose purely by chance. Evidently when the first railway tracks were laid to quarries up North, they were laid on old Roman, timber wagon-tracks that had that gauge. The 'Six-foot' is the six feet space between these and the next pair, usually creating one 'Up' line (to London) and one 'Down' line (away from London).

On mainline sections there is often second pair of tracks for fast trains, so between the two sets of lines, is a ten feet space – the 'Ten-foot' - on one side, the two Up lines to London, and the other, the Down lines. Finally, at both sides of all the tracks is an empty space called the Cess, often used as a workmen's walkway. And all that was just the beginning of the terms we had to get hold of *toute suite*.

These first contracts were obtained during the period immediately after the railway had been privatised. With so much internal reorganisation taking place, it was a probably not the best time for outsiders to get into railway work, but that's how it was.

In the period leading up to it, the nationalised British Rail (BR) was assessed to be over-manned and had been told by the government to reduce its staffing levels to make it more attractive to private investors. So in its wisdom, they had offered generous voluntary redundancy packages to try to achieve this. The immediate result was that the higher paid and of course longest serving - most capable employees, took the money and ran. Some, with experience and expertise, didn't retire to the country nut established private 'support companies', and now supplied labour and technical know-how to Railtrack on a profit-making contract basis. Into their shoes back on the railway – at all levels – stepped many people who were new to the railway and to its complexities. And that was the situation we met when we moved in.

It is often underestimated how much the human factor affects the running of such large organisations. Many staff had been 'railway people' man and boy. It had become a vocation, a way of life, and a unique railway culture had grown up, where mates worked, felt at home and everyone was dedicated to make it succeed. Now, together with privatisation and dismemberment into different areas, much of that personal experience and expertise was lost. It was like throwing out the baby with the bathwater.

It was probably true that the railways were over-manned and that there were inefficient practices and some slacking. But all in all, despite lack of investment by the private railway companies between the wars, and successive governments ever since the Fifties, the tracks and rolling stock were kept in a pretty good state precisely through the dedication and expertise of the employees.

In much the same way, despite ancient infrastructure and outdated signalling controls on London Underground – some systems then still used radio valves! – dedicated staff managed somehow to keep the tube trains running with few hitches. Luckily, as we discovered during the course of our contracts, there were just sufficient old-timers left in the new Railtrack set-up to keep the system working too. But now there were also many new people, unfamiliar with the whole system, and to whom it was just another job.

Previously, all maintenance - especially track work, was carried out by experienced staff, directly employed British Rail. Now, it had been parcelled out, by competitive tender to sub-contractors – who in turn employed the cheapest labour they could get. So by the time we came in, little of the old spirit survived. It also appeared that to keep costs down and improve profitability, privatised Railtrack was keeping those maintenance works to an absolute minimum. Ladbroke Grove, Hatfield, Potters Bar and others, were accidents just waiting to happen.

With Railtrack then embarking on a large investment programme, ours and other large construction companies didn't want to miss out on the opportunities. So, despite having to contend with a mixture of a few ex-BR men and new, private, projects managers, our company dipped its toes into railway infrastructure renewal and maintenance.

My first contract, for several million pounds at a major London terminus, was large enough for me to be stationed permanently on site with my surveyor, and we were allotted a disused part of the station yard in which to site our huts.

Prior to commencing work, I went first to look for the Station Master, once that high chief whose word once ran as a king's edict in every station. Except that he no longer existed! Instead there was one person in charge of the station buildings, another responsible for the shops and restaurants on the concourse, and a duty station – or duty services – manager (DSM) dealing with the railway infrastructure.

He dealt with the nuts and bolts of the platforms and getting the trains in and out of the station, and of the three people required to maintain a three, eight-hour shift, 24 hour operation, often one or two of the DSM's might be completely new to the railway. (We soon found out that on the railways, similar to the armed forces, speaking in acronyms was the normal thing, (though this has crept into the construction industry too: CDM, BIM, ISO, QA, BIM, etc., etc., - and the list grows with each issue of 'Construction Manager' magazine.)

At another, smaller terminus where I worked, there was no DSM at all. The station was run by one of the new railway companies and the man in charge was a 'commercial manager'. His main interest was to increase the income from letting out concessions to retailers on the station forecourt. We also found that now, many of the new Railtrack project managers, surveyors and technical support people on our contracts were from agencies, and having jobs only for the duration of the contract, were – to put it gently - of varying competence.

Before being allowed to work in the stations or along the line, all of us involved in the contract – from Managing Director to sub-contractors to labourers, had to acquire Personal Track Safety (PTS) certificates. This involved a day's training, familiarising ourselves with the jargon and safety procedures that had evolved over a century and a half to ensure safe working. As part of that, we were also taken down onto the track, including learning to cross the live rail without getting electrocuted in the process, and by which Designated Route we were allowed to cross the tracks at a station. Railway workers who ignored these routes were immediately dismissed.

Perhaps the most unfamiliar – and onerous – procedure was the need to reconcile 'Possessions' with our contract programme.

A 'Possession', is obtaining permission to shut down a section of track or a platform in order to get some work done on or alongside it. Now programming large or lengthy construction projects is difficult enough in itself, but with much of our work being on the platforms and close to the line, we now had to take account of these too. Except that these Possessions' times were completely outside of our control.

Even if they had been requested months in advance, nothing could be guaranteed until a week beforehand when the 'Weekly Operating Notice' (WON), was issued. This thin A5 booklet details all the possessions in the area, by signal or points' numbers – so we had to become conversant with all those around our workplace. (We also had to find a Railtrack person who had a copy of the booklet). If our requested possession wasn't in that book, any work programmed for that week in that area had to be cancelled.

A further problem was that even if authorised in the weekly booklet, if there were emergency works – even fifty miles further up that same line, a possession could be cancelled at short notice. So the sub-contractors and specialists waiting to go in that date had to be cancelled and re-programmed and another possession requested – which of course was not without problems, as the operatives themselves might already be committed to another station with its own pre-arranged possessions. In short, the whole programme could be shot to pieces in a few nights, and would have to be completely reorganised.

So each week, it was vital to obtain a copy of the following week's WON booklet and it took us a while to find out from where to obtain it. After a while, surprisingly, every Friday my surveyor at Kings Cross – who normally preferred sorting out accounts in the site hut - would disappear way down the end of Platform One and return some time later, booklet in hand. Curious, one day I went with him, only to discover in a nondescript Victorian brick building by the signals' gantry, a mature but very attractive lady who ran that office. It took him a while to live that down, but I didn't say a word to the others back at head office, so – as we say - he owed me one.

Anyway, once we had obtained notice of possessions in our work area, if they didn't contradict our programme, gangs of sub-contractors concerned would be lined up for that night's work – usually between midnight and 5.00 am. To make doubly sure, we usually checked with the local, main signal box or the station control room as well, no simple matter at first, because for security reasons, they were often locked from the inside. Eventually we got to know the digital lock codes or designated telephone in each station – but that took time, and all this proved to be a very rapid learning curve.

To ensure safety, every Possession had to have a railway, qualified 'Person in Charge of Possession' (PICOP) present. In addition, all work on or near the line itself also had to have a qualified 'Person in Charge of Works' (PICOW) on site, and these experienced railway men were invaluable. At the prescribed hour, they would set warning barriers and lights across the track and fix three detonators on the rails some distance ahead, so that a train approaching too near would set them off with a loud bang. And of course, all of these had to be paid for and priced into the contract.

In the actual work section, the electrical current had to be isolated too – and prearranged to be tied in with the possessions. These 'Isolations' were carried out by a separate company – at around a thousand pounds per shift, so if the possession was called off at the last moment, say through an emergency down the line, all those costs – and those of the subcontractors standing down - would be incurred too.

All this proved to be a steep and expensive learning curve for us. Given these costs and their occasional unpredictability, many contractors became wary of taking on this work without an arrangement for payment of lost time. At the time though, all these were all unknown factors to us.

A further feature that we had to take into account,

was that most London termini are Grade I or II listed buildings. Most of them are wonderful examples of Victorian architecture and engineering – just look at the steel arches and brickwork in Kings Cross or St. Pancras, or experience the charm of Marylebone. Therefore all cable runs, ducts or holes had to be approved by an English Heritage architect before work could begin. A further complication was that having mainly been built at least a hundred years previously, many of the structural drawings once filed away had been lost or destroyed during the Blitz in the Second World War.

If that wasn't enough, following privatisation, in the Eastern Region reorganisation, previously indexed drawings from many different stations had been collected and transferred en-mass to York to be stored in a huge warehouse. There, in the shadow of the ancient city walls, with the kind assistance of the staff there, I managed to extract from the chaos a few relevant drawings for our work at Kings Cross. They are probably still sorting out the rest...

Even when we had the old drawings, finding our way around the innards of the station buildings where we needed to run miles of cabling and ducting, wasn't simple either. Having been built in and era of coal-powered steam, cheap labour and deference to one's superiors, the old terminus administration blocks held over a hundred rooms. These had once housed the myriad officials, clerks, office boys, porters, waiters, food and wine stores, etc. of the Victorian Railways system.

After much searching, we would obtain the right key to a long-locked door and discover what had been a grand managerial office complete with mahogany panelling, corniced ceilings and marble fireplaces – often in completely empty wings. Absolutely deserted for decades, they were now valuable real estate in the centre of London and other cities. Little wonder then, that Railtrack's property portfolio was probably worth more than it's entire track system – which is probably why they bought it.

Beneath all these offices were endless store-rooms, Victorian kitchens, convoluted tunnels and corridors and narrow ducts for gas and water mains, through which we had to run our new pipes and cables and Fire Alarm systems. Some hadn't been trodden in since the demise of steam and were dark, sooty rat-runs – literally. In one office wing, the original 1860's lime plaster had used animal hair, which could have carried anthrax. So we had to sheet it off and send samples to the government's Porton Down chemical warfare laboratories for analysis. Luckily, three weeks later we got the all clear.

Rats were also an ever-present hazard, especially since they can carry Leptospirosis. This is a fatal disease whose early symptoms are just like an ordinary flu, which, by the time they'd become serious, could be too late. So whether it was a huge unused tunnel at Paddington, or the network of corridors and cellars under Stratford, working conditions were sometimes more like the backdrop for a Hammer Horror Film, than for building works.

Much of our work involved installing fire-safety measures, new fire-doors and walls, safety alarms, emergency lighting and Public Address (PA) systems.

Unfortunately, Mainline stations have the worst possible acoustic combination: hard, smooth reflective surfaces at platform level that completely distorted any sound, and huge, high, vaulted roof spaces into which the rest of the message disappears. Older people will recall the absolutely unintelligible, reverberating loudspeaker announcements on most stations. So in an attempt to make emergency warnings and announcements clearer, we carried out detailed acoustic tests with specialists to design the best system.

The solution arrived at was to have many small loudspeakers at lower level. This of course required miles of fireproof cabling which, in the Listed stations had to be run as unobtrusively as possible on the walls and then all painted to match the background.

Of course, all these systems are fine as long as there is electric power. The horror of having a station full of people when the power failed, prompted the designers to install back-up power that would keep the lights, speakers etc., working for a few hours to prevent accidents and give time to evacuate the station.

This came in the form of large banks of batteries, kept permanently at full charge with a trickle charging system and they had to be housed somewhere dry yet accessible. In most stations, there were cavernous underground areas, but most of there were damp and unsuitable. At Kings Cross, it was decided to utilise a large room under the clocks in the main tower. This required a special hydraulic-lift apparatus to hoist the heavy batteries and chargers fifty feet up to a small doorway, and slide them in. Since this was over the main concourse, it had to be done at night – and took the best part of it.

Anyone visiting or using Kings Cross station today would have no idea what it was like only two decades ago. The whole area is now a vibrant commercial and meeting hub, with cafes, high-rise housing and offices. At the rear, behind platforms 9-11, there is now a roadway and offices leading to Kings Place and a spruced up Regents Canal with broad terraces in front of St Martins college.

When we set up site, this whole area was a was a cinder covered wasteland adjacent to the old Gasometers, where old loading ramps still carried Victorian notices for milk and other deliveries 'from the country'.

An unusual work hazard was that for many years, the station was in the middle of the noted Red Light district. When working at night we used to joke that like the Harriers in the Falklands Campaign, the foreman had to count the men out and count them all back again at the end of each shift. The derelict, then soot-coated German Gymnasium - where we had to install arm-thick, heavy electric cables, crawling under the eaves - has been cleaned up and is now a smart restaurant.

As these railway contracts progressed – and with huge, old stations like Waterloo, Victoria, Paddington and Kings Cross the problems were huge too – we gradually grew to understand the systems and limitations and work within them. Needless to say, there was a steep and expensive learning curve, not helped by the ad-hoc nature of the specific Railtrack 'project management' systems with their equally huge amounts of paperwork and new, often temporary staff, all then in a process of transition.

Working on the London Underground (LUL), proved

to be even more onerous. Unlike the surface railways where trains can be diverted onto alternative tracks, each line has only one track. So any maintenance or refurbishment work on the platforms, corridors or in the tunnels on that line has to be done in the closed hours – usually from one to five in the morning.

You can always tell if an underground station is being refurbished, when passing by at night. Just when the station and the surrounding area is becoming almost deserted of people, a fleet of cars, vans and lorries begins to assemble in the nearby streets, men sitting in cabs or leaning against bonnets, downing a last cup of coffee or a sandwich, waiting for the off. For there is nothing they can do until the LUL supervisor, who's word is God in these matters, has checked that the rails' current has been switched off, and comes out to allow the workers in - usually around 1.00 am.

Knowing that they all have to be out again by 5.00 am, at the supervisor's signal the whole area comes alive with men and tools and materials – mainly sub-contractors on a price – all hurrying down the corridors and escalators and eager to start as soon as possible. Given the time taken to get down and up again, they are lucky to put in four hours of actual work – though the men get paid for a full night work shift. Which incidentally is why when, say, re-tiling alongside a station platform, travellers can see empty patches successively left for the following nights. Any work that is liable to take longer than four hours, like changing rails, means closing the line at weekends. And with the Underground, like the railways, having been starved of investment over the years, that will probably continue to occur long into the future.

We were among the first contractors to 'cut their teeth' on this kind of work. The unusually long periods of working nights and weekends took its toll on the men and their families. Some gave it up for that reason and there was more of a turnover than usual. Slowly but surely though, our site-agents and sub-contractors learned the systems, grew accustomed to, and took account of, the specific nature of the work.

So I never got the chance to fulfil the little boy's childhood dream and drive a steam engine, but I suppose it was the next best thing – a once in a lifetime experience to be involved in 'Working on the Railway'.

ARS GRATIA ARTIST

Dennis was the site agent on several of our museum contracts. Artistic appreciation though was not one of his strong points.

This became apparent one day when I happened to call on site whilst we were converting a Georgian house. One of the carpenters was tapping screw-plugs into the lounge wall for a new dado rail. It was a party wall.

In a pause in the hammering, suddenly came a gentle knock on the half-open front door. Now on a building site no one knocks – certainly not gently – they just walk in. Curious, I went out to see. On the doorstep stood a neatly dressed, diminutive, grey-haired lady.

'Excuse me,' she said – quite politely, I felt afterwards considering what had happened, 'I'm afraid you've just knocked a valuable painting of my wall.'

Immediately, all work stopped and Dennis, the chippie and I all trooped round with her to next door. It being Hampstead, I expected to find a Turner or Constable lying on her lounge floor, my head beginning to spin at the size of the probable insurance claim and whether it would hit the local press – everyone in the area reads the Hampstead & Highgate Express.

The woman pointed to her settee. Resting on the cushions was a small collage of what looked like four painted, hardboard triangles on a stippled brown boarding, a simple frame. Three had become detached. Evidently, our chippie's tapping the plugs into the party wall had knocked the work off its hook – which was actually just a small nail.

Gently, I remarked that a valuable work like that

might surely have had a decent fixing.

'Well it's been there for eight years,' she said sharply, 'and never fallen off yet.'

So I said no more, apart from assuring her that our insurance would deal with it.

'In the meantime, I added, 'could you get a quotation for the restoration work?'

'Here. No need for that,' said Dennis stepping forward. 'My chippie, John, can soon fix them back with a bit of contact adhesive.

The woman froze and for a moment I thought she was going to have a heart seizure. Slowly relaxing, she said stiffly:

'This is one of Eric Tomkins' – or some name like that – mature works,' adding, 'and the last valuation was at twenty five thousand pounds.'

Dennis opened his mouth to give his opinion on contemporary art but I managed to catch his eye and he got the message. On the way back to the site though, he couldn't refrain from what he thought of the collage. And in his no-nonsense way, at the time I felt he might have a point. Either way, I didn't have the heart to inform him later, that a specialist restorer had taken four thousand pounds for the repair. Nor that our insurance had paid up without further questioning. Either way, when both he and the chippies went to work on one of our museum contracts, I had no need to stress how careful they had to be.

Our company was on the list of contractors approved for government and public institutions work, and our department had obtained onto a contract to completely re-roof one of the large galleries at the Tate Britain, Millbank.

When we went to view the work, as we were being taken along a rear corridor, the museum surveyor noticed Dennis looking down at four small, grubby, bronze plaques that were leaning against the foot of the wall.

'So,' he asked with a smile. 'What do you think those are worth?' Dennis stopped for a moment then scratched his chin.

'Well, I suppose my plumber might give you about hundred and fifty quid for scrap,' he muttered, adding, 'if he can find someone who does that stuff.

The surveyor coughed – choked would be more apt.

'Hundred and fifty thousand, more like it,' he muttered.

We were looking at the rear faces of four Matisse bronzes!'

In most museums, there seems hardly a period when some contractor or other is not working there. Apart from the regular maintenance work that those grand Victorian edifices require – some of it quite large scale – either a gallery is being altered or a special exhibition installed. Something is always going on. As a result, the rear access roads – what we call the arse-end of the museum – are always jammed full of sub-contractors' vans and cars. Unlike many modern buildings, the Victorian architects seemed to realise the importance of decent access and working space needed for the upkeep of these buildings, and although always busy, there was usually space to park and unload.

At the Victoria and Albert museum, so much work is constantly in process and with so many operatives booking in every morning, a special 'Victorian style' entrance hut has been built at the service road gates to deal with them. Between half-past seven and eight in the morning, there was quite often a queue of tradesmen having their passes checked that could keep you waiting for twenty minutes or more. Later, during the period when entrance charges were introduced, at times it seemed that more workmen were going in at this side entrance than there were visitors through the main entrance. And it was at the Victoria and Albert Museum that we had this contract to remodel the new Indian Gallery.

When I noted the proximity of priceless sculptures and paintings to our work area, mindful of the Hampstead art-work, on every site visit, I strolled through the adjacent galleries, noting where objects were fixed to walls backing onto ours and briefing the agent and the men. But no matter how many times I'd observed them and warned everyone, the activities of some of the more casual workmen gave me nightmares. It was a nerve racking experience for example, to watch the scaffolders casually carrying a couple of twenty foot, steel poles down a gallery between rows of glass cases containing irreplaceable objets d'art. To give them their due though, they did seem to know the score and their apparent nonchalant manner was misleading.

Our main problem on this contract were the preparatory demolitions. The contract specification specified that all demolitions and drilling were to be carried out without any knocking or vibration. By bad luck, the main wall to which we had to fix exhibition racking, was behind a breezeblock wall that had been erected some time on the past for some unknown reason. It easily could have been knocked down in a day or so with Kango hammers and hand tools but on the other side of this main wall, were two ornate mediaeval altar screens. So we had to use a diamond-core drilling – an expensive and time consuming process, cutting innumerable rows of 100 millimetre holes – like making huge perforations in a sheet of postage stamps, then gently easing out the sections between. It took over a week and a half . . .

Even with a regime of constant awareness and checking, there were incidents that gave me sleepless nights. Like 'the day of the great dust cloud'.

Across the site entrance to our work gallery, we had installed an air-lock door, using double screens of heavy polythene sheeting. With fine dust from knocking down and re-building internal block walls, everyone was instructed to make sure that the first screen was closed before opening the second. We'd been warned that the museum curators would take a dim view if there any dust drifted outside. Since we were after repeat work there, we were strict in enforcing this. So I was gutted to receive an irate telephone call from the head of the department one afternoon, summoning me to meet him immediately. 'Dust everywhere!' he'd snarled down the phone.

It appeared that a joinery delivery had arrived just as a new exhibition pantechnicons were queuing up outside in the rear access road. A delivery of timber and boards for our site had just arrived, and was given just fifteen minutes to offload before having to move on. Panicking, the driver ran in to warn Dennis, who equally panicking it seems, rushed out with half a dozen workmen through the air lock doors. By chance – or by the inevitable Sod's Law – concrete drillers were cutting in chases for conduits in the old Victorian walls, creating a cloud of dust. As the last two men hurried after Dennis, they didn't wait for the first screen to close behind them before plunging through the second. So with a howling draught blowing down the corridor from the open, rear-loading door, a cloud of lime-plaster dust was wafted out and down two long galleries of classical sculpture!

After the phone call, I immediately dropped everything and jumped into my car to head for the V&A. When I arrived, the curator of the gallery was dancing a jig up and down the corridors, wiping dust with his finger to show me just what had happened and calling down fire and brimstone on builders in general. Apparently, lime-plaster dust has a deleterious effect on marble and other fine finishes. 'If it is not cleaned off immediately,' he snapped, 'it starts a corrosive chemical action. Irreparable!'

'I'll get all the men to clean it off as soon as we've unloaded the joinery,' I said amidst profuse apologies.

'What?' he yelled, 'I would let your men anywhere near those objects! And if it's not cleaned off soon, I will make an estimate of the damage.' I was already totting up how many noughts do you add to the costs of repairing damage to priceless, ancient Greek sculptures? Couldn't even begin to estimate the possible insurance claims. Panic. Panic.

'Well, how do you usually clean the galleries?' I asked.

'We have our own specialist contract cleaners who know what they are doing. Early morning,' he snapped, 'and they have already gone home. And anyway,' he added, 'I haven't a budget for extra cleaning.'

'Look,' said quickly. 'bring them back as an emergency – adding quickly, 'and we shall cover all the costs.'

'Oh. Very well then,' he said, surprised and suddenly relaxing. 'I'll go and phone them. But I they will have to receive their payment by next week!'

'Of course,' I promised. 'I'll bring the cheque to you myself.' And he hurried away through the residual dust cloud to telephone.

The bill came to quite a few hundred pounds, and on a contract for nearly a million my surveyor hardly noticed – but it could have been disastrous and we might have been removed from their approved list.

The following morning, assembling all the men together behind the polythene sheeting, I read them – and Dennis – the riot act. And we had no more incidents.

Despite the stress and regulations' minutae, museum work had its compensations. One was that there was usually a warm buffet where you could find a decent cup of coffee on a freezing winter's morning. It was never cheap and there was always the bustle of tourists and school parties, but compared to the dirt and hassle of the site, it was peace itself and where you could have quiet conversation with the site agent. It was also a place where we could meet informally and chat with the curators or the architect, which was always helpful in understanding each other's problems and improving relations – especially as we generally bought the coffee and croissants.

The other compensation was the chance to spend time in the museum galleries themselves, something one never seemed to find time to do otherwise. After a late afternoon meeting or a long day's site visit, there was usually an hour or so to closing time and an opportunity to take in a bit of "culture" – and for free – since most museums had installed entrance charges those days.

Another memorable museum project was the creation of a one of the first, specialist DNA extraction laboratory at the Natural History Museum in South Kensington. Using their huge collection of specimens going back millions of years, they hoped top extract traces of DNA, which would invaluable to research on Evolution.

The laboratory was to be formed out of a large, disused storage basement that happened to be beneath the huge Sperm Whale model – under which every child once stood in awe, so it was called 'The Whale Basement'.

In adjacent areas were cupboards and chests of drawers full of cardboard boxes and glass containers of specimens that had been collected over the last hundred and fifty years from across the world. It was from these and similar storage, that the museum hoped to extract samples for research. So a light touch was required by all concerned.

The laboratory required a completely uncluttered floor space that would be a sterile area. So the specification demanded that all the electrical carcassing, air-conditioning and heating and ventilation plant and ducting, be installed at high level, out of the way. This was to carried on timber mezzanine floor, supported by a lightweight steelwork lattice, complete with a waterproof membrane to ensure that no drips would fall through to the workspace below. All this was to be slung from steel rods drilled into the concrete ceiling of the ground floor above.

To avoid disturbance to the museum visitors, much of the drilling and noisy work had to be carried out in the early hours of the morning. During down times, we sometimes wandered up an internal service staircase to take a peep at the exhibits above, wondering what would happen if, through the vibration from our work, the enormous hulk of that whale ever came down on the floor above our heads . . .

In an adjacent gallery, the exhibits showed the ascent of man from the apes, which gave Dennis the opportunity to voice comparisons with one of the scaffolders who'd just tipped out a sack of steel couplings on his newly screeded floor.

The intended DNA investigations would evidently use quite corrosive chemicals and these required especially resistant, bespoke laboratory benches. These were all being pre-cast somewhere up in Lancashire from a proprietary, rigid-plastic material. Once set, this plastic could only be cut with specialist diamond-tipped saws and drills.

The old walls were not exactly at right angles however, but the benches had been fabricated dead-square. So the ends of a few benches and had to be skew-cut to fit, and even with this specialist equipment, cutting the ends into the walls was laborious and time consuming. At the end of the job, I picked up two discarded jig-saw blades coated with diamond grit. Perhaps the ultimate nail-file for the woman who had everything?

By the time we had finished, a dark, dusty basement that hadn't been used since Victoria had been transformed into a pristine, specialist, state-of-the-art laboratory.

By chance, many years later at a Royal Society conference, I met the head researcher at the Natural History Museum asked about the laboratory. It had been just the beginning, he said and now they had two more, larger ones and had done valuable work sequencing ancient DNA. So I felt pleased that we had contributed something to that new science.

A few years after that, we had a maintenance and repair contract at the British Newspaper Library in Colindale. This housed copies of practically every newspaper ever printed in English from when they began in the eighteenth century. Owing to the wear and tear of the paper by researchers over the years however, the Library was into an enormous project to copy them onto to microfilm before it was too late.

Although anyone is allowed come into the special reading room and order a specific newspaper to read and research, the newspapers themselves were stored in bound volumes on racks, in huge hangars that were closed to the public.

On site visits or after site meetings, in a quiet moment or two after work hours, I sometimes took the opportunity to wander through these racks. Amongst the tomes of newspapers from past and present centuries, I could and amuse myself in reading say the Limerick Recorder of 1893 or similar, whose entire back page would be taken up with a court case about the damages sought through someone's donkey having wandered into a neighbour's cornfield! Or discover hundred-year-old newspapers from the Raj carrying news of the latest arrivals from the Home Country . . . I imagined one could immerse oneself for years and not loose interest.

In a rolling programme, the Library was well into the microfilming programme, so that researchers would have ready access through these films, and so avoid even more damage to the originals. To do this, in another area of the library, I found half a dozen women, many from the local Asian community, standing at desks and patiently turning the pages of these yellowed, dog-eared newspapers in order to microfilm them. Day after day, they turn a page and press a pedal that activates the camera, then turn the next page and press the pedal. And so on – day after day, to earn a living.

It made me put into perspective the times we would moan about this contract or that, or this client or architect – whether it was all worth the stress and hassle. But then, having let off steam, would console ourselves that at least it wasn't like manning the Ford assembly line at Dagenham. After this though, I felt that now I'd seen a labour that could be even more soul-destroying . . .

More than anything however, those museum contracts gave us the satisfaction of working to preserve or enhance a national monument or a priceless cultural heritage, and not just throwing up some commercial development that would be re-hashed or demolished in a few years when working methods and technology had moved on. Like the five, container lorry-loads (I exaggerate not!) of gold-tipped, copper, computer cabling we sent to the tip, from one such office conversion near

Baker Street, since it wouldn't do for the new client's IT systems . . .

And as for the Matisse bronzes, the next day when we passed along that corridor, they had been removed. Perhaps the curator had been worried that they would indeed end up for scrap in the back of the plumber's van...

THE SILVER SCREEN

For a while, I was working with a Company that had a running contract with some of the large leisure companies, like EMI, Rank and others, and at the time, they were converting cinemas. In the Eighties, someone had discovered that the film industry could be snatched back from the jaws of television, by getting rid of the huge, stuffy old cinemas and creating two or three smaller auditoriums with modern décor and showing a choice of films.

This particular conversion was in a Midland town and it was nearly midnight. Alan, our assistant director, who often visited the sites, was stamping to and fro across the cinema foyer, his sharp face even sharper than usual, smoking his way through a packet of cigarettes.

'Can't get any decision out of the Old Man,' he snapped

'The Old Man', was an architect who specialised in the leisure industry. He was a dab hand at converting the old art-deco cinemas into multi-screen modern ones or, when the location demanded, remodelling them into spruced-up, Bingo halls. And the decorations' schedule was all in his head.

Although the overall schemes and technical problems were similar, each conversion was a one-off, depending on the structure and size of the original cinema. And that night, just two weeks away to the grand opening, the decorators were being held up waiting for his decision on the final decorations' schedule to the entrance foyers and corridors, and were threatening to leave site.

'He's irked because he won't get his usual tonight. Rachel's kid is sick so she can't come up from London,' Alan grunted. It appeared that Rachel, an attractive single mum, was one of the secretaries. She and he had this thing going whenever we had an out of town contract or occasionally – if he could make the arrangements – in London.

Most of the cinemas we were converting had been built as prestigious, art deco 'Picture Palaces' in the Thirties. They all had an extremely convoluted series of escape staircases, winding and climbing through the thick walls around the auditorium. For the first few days of every contract, half the men seemed to get lost and had to retrace their steps until familiarising themselves with the building. Once I became so completely lost myself trying to locate the electricians working in one of the old toilets, that I swore that next time I would take Ariadne's ball of twine with me to find my way out.

The general scheme at each location was similar: dividing the large, main auditorium into two smaller cinemas by a soundproof partition down the centre, each new one fitted with a suspended ceiling to reduce the height. If there was a large balcony or circle, a third, upstairs cinema could be formed by enclosing it at the front to separate it from the main auditorium, and of course each new cinema was provided with a new stage, screen and seating.

A vital aspect of the conversion was to preserve reasonable sight lines from most of the new seats – though in the smaller ones I sometimes wondered whether those in the front rows ever suffered a slipped-disc after a night's viewing. The other important factor was to fit in as large a screen as possible – though they were always much smaller than the original. And of course everything had to satisfy the local Building Inspector and the Fire Officer before it would be allowed to open. Which occasionally was problematic, as at one large West London cinema.

The old balcony area was quite short, but there was plenty of space and height in the main auditorium to extend it, and so install a third screen upstairs with new seating. The plan was to extend the balcony out over the stalls with a new, suspended concrete floor. This would be supported on heavy steelwork, the ends concreted into the side walls.

Our problem was that the slope of the main auditorium made it hazardous to use mechanical hoists. So after all the seats had been removed, we manhandled the heavy steel beams into the stalls, then raised them into position, one end at a time, using a 'scaffold stick'. Essentially this was a telegraph pole with a block-and-tackle assembly attached near the top. In today's increasingly mechanised construction world it would be a museum piece, but in this awkward, enclosed space, it served our purpose admirably.

After the steelwork had all been bolted together, and the ends concreted into the side walls, we called in the local District Surveyor, or DS as he is affectionately known - and the nearest thing to God in the construction world - to give his stamp of approval. (as it is said: when a DS died and went up to heaven, as the pearly gates opened he yelled: 'who's that sitting in my chair!').

Since our retained structural engineer was well qualified and experienced in this kind of work, usually this inspection was just a formality. This time however, after glancing at the drawings and then at the steelwork, the DS frowned.

'Can't rely just on those bolted steelwork connections,' he said. 'Need some supporting cleats,' - which are small angle-iron pieces.

Well, we were already a week behind programme and to try to catch up, men were already laying out the Holorib metal decking and steel reinforcement-mesh for the new concrete floor that would rest on these beams. In addition, concrete lorries had been ordered for the following day. Alan, who had quite a bit of engineering experience himself, began to argue that surely the bolted connections were sufficient.

'Look,' said the DS quietly. 'I'm just not satisfied. Okay?' Then as he turned to go added, 'see that new New Shopping Centre down the road. It's still not open after a year because the builders didn't listen to me!' So after urgent telephone calls, the steel fabricators came back and worked all through the night, drilling and bolting on the new cleats so that we could pour the concrete the next morning.

A similar hiccup happened in Sheffield. Again we had to construct an additional high-level floor, but this time Brendan, the sub-contractor, had used temporary plywood decking on which to cast the concrete. As he had worked with us reliably on a number of contracts, we just left him to it.

When the floor had been poured however, the Building Inspector happened to drop by on his rounds. (In some towns he is called the District Surveyor, but more often, the Building Inspector). Two days later, I received a cryptic letter at head office. Could we explain to him 'the structural significance of the plywood trapped between the steelwork flange and the concrete?' I loved his sense of humour.

In their rush, or thoughtlessness, Brendan's men had left pieces of the temporary plywood decking on the flanges of steel beam, trapped by the new concrete. Brendan wasn't laughing though when his men had to hack it all out, and dry-pack with sand and cement and steel spacers, all at his own expense.

Although each conversion was a bespoke job, because of the specialised, yet repetitive elements in the work, we tried to use the same sub-contractors who knew exactly what to do and when. The carpenters, John and Damien for example, were invariably part of the same band of merry, country lads from East Anglia. They travelled to wherever the site was and slept in local digs – or in the back of their van, working long hours, usually two or three weeks at a time, then going home to their families for a long weekend. The other men joked that once home, they would be too knackered to take advantage of conjugal life anyway – though in more colourful terms.

Similarly, the plasterers, Brian and his gang from Romford, the upholsterers from South London, flooring contractors from Brixton, plumbers, electricians, and Londoners John, Len and Alf - the decorators, all became part of the team.

Despite the often conflicting demands of space and plant, they were used to working alongside one another with give and take, and despite the occasional fierce oath, were accustomed to the crazy pace of work to finish for the Celebrity opening each time – because inevitably there was one. Above all, despite the stress and the occasional panic, as the men knew one another, there was always much good humoured ribbing.

One of the heartiest - though most painful – laughs, was when the electricians were overhauling the old air-conditioning system of the Thirties' cinema in Northampton. Someone inadvertently switched the polarity of the fan cables, so when it was started up again to test, more than forty years of dust and nicotine shot out into the auditorium, sending everyone coughing and spluttering in a mad rush for the exit doors and into the fresh air outside...

In every cinema, the very first specialist on site was usually old Harry, the upholsterer. He was an elderly man who, we joked, must have been in the game since Queen Victoria, always wearing a long overcoat that looked as ancient. Since the new auditoriums were inevitably a different shape to the original and in many instances had new raised floors, all the seats had to be removed and re-set in new rows. Having provided seating and snogging over a few generations, many also needed re-springing and recovering. So it was a good time to refurbish the lot, often with new fabric to match the Old Man's decor.

It often took a few days to unbolt the seats and load them into Harry's furniture van, to be sorted out in his workshop somewhere in Bermondsey, and returned nearer the end of the contract. Once they had been removed, the carpet layer came in to measure up for new carpets. Occasionally, for a prestige site, the leisure company wanted its logo outlined in the new carpets and these had to be especially woven to suit. In general, though, we were on a tight, fixed-price contract and the new carpet design and colour just matched the new decor.

Once everything had been stripped out, if there were no structural works, the next stage was erecting the dividing walls between the new Screens One and Two. This posed a problem since they had to be lightweight, yet acoustically sound-proof – a kind of negation of one of the basic laws of physics. And sound is the most penetrative of all the elements - even a hairline-crack will transmit music.

To achieve this, three overlapping layers of plasterboard were fixed to each side of six-inch wide, Jumbo metal studding, and the hollow space between the boards packed with a 'Stillite', fibrous acoustic padding. The final layer of plasterboard was taper-edged and dry-lined ready for wall-papering, all wet trades being reduced to a minimum to save time.

A major problem in the soundproofing works, were the junctions between the old walls and ceilings. Often we had to cut through the existing, ornamental plaster ceiling to reach the solid underside of the balcony or the old structural ceiling up high. And if the existing timber floor had to remain and there was a void underneath, again this had to be cut through to allow the new partition to meet the solid concrete floor beneath, and all the junctions were sealed with a special, acoustic mastic.

Alan took a professional pride especially in this part of the work. When our job was finished and sound tests carried out, not a whisper could be heard from one auditorium to the other. You can always tell a cheap cinema conversion – never one of ours - by the sound creeping in from the adjacent auditorium during a quiet part of the film.

Difficult problems were always posed by the old ventilation system, especially if it was being part re-used. Steel ducting passing from one new auditorium to the other would carry sound, so they had to be cut off and re-routed, not forgetting automatic fire-dampers at each wall they passed through, which would close when the fire alarm was set off. All the ventilation system and dampers, like the exit doors etc., had to meet the local Fire Officer's approval – another official whose word was as God's - and rightly so.

After the partitions were finished and sealed, the carpenters came in to install the new floors in timber and plywood decking, often in the form of terraces to create good sight lines to the screen. Invariably, when the local Building Inspector turned up, he would stamp or jump his way along one or two terraces to test their stability, while the chippies looked on and smiled. They were always rock solid.

Managing the contract often called for night-time supervision and unusual hours to fit in with the tight work schedules. This usually involved me in long trips up the motorway in the dead of night, on the way back fighting like mad to stay awake – and occasionally finding that I'd crossed lanes without noticing, and was almost on the verge.

Once, at about three in the morning, as I was coming down the M1 from a cinema in Nottingham, police cars were drawn up across the two outside lanes, lights flashing. Ahead, a car lay on its roof and two others nearby were on their sides. A fourth was half-way up the adjacent grass bank, its doors wide open. Nearby, a small group of dazed-looking people were sitting up on the grass slope and looking on, silent, obviously in shock. Behind me an ambulance was approaching fast, sounding its siren and lights flashing.

In the faint moonlight, as the traffic slowly edged past in the slow lane and hard shoulder, it was like a scene out of a dream or a surreal film. After that, whenever I felt my eyes closing, I would pull in to the side with flashers on for a minute or two then head for next service station for a quick shut-eye and coffee. No contract was worth dying for.

While all this new construction work was going on, the electrical and mechanical services' specialists would be sorting out their work. But before they could even commence, they had to trace the existing ones that wove in and out through the enormously thick brick walls, and up and down staircases and corridors and into fire exits and lobbies. In many of the cinemas, falling audiences over the years had resulted in little or no maintenance, and at some cinemas the wiring had become downright dangerous. Creating new ventilation duct runs, or refurbishing the toilets' plumbing also called for much lateral thinking and expertise and at time I was amazed at the patience of these specialist workers as they went up and down, and in and out of old lobbies and corridors, again and again, sussing out the best route for their pipe or cable runs.

Nearing the end of the contract, it was time to re-model the front foyer with new kiosks and counters, and now everywhere it was the turn of the decorators. Which was where the Old Man and his design flair really came into its own.

He used gaudy 'Bromel' theatrical colours that we

rarely come across in general contracting but in the cinemas, amazingly they seemed totally in place once the whole lot was finished. Sometimes the old cornices and moulding were kept and highlighted, at others, painted black to melt into the background.

Another problem we faced in some cinemas was that the ornate ceiling had to be retained as part of a Listed Building notice. So access for redecorating it, often at fifty feet above the sloping auditorium floor, was not simple.

In many of these old cinemas, the original builders had foreseen this and had installed a system of shackles and pulleys fixed the roof steelwork and hidden above hatches in the fibrous-plaster ceiling. From these, a floating scaffold platform could be slung on cables and winched up to about eight feet below the ceiling.

It was a strange feeling to climb up and feel the whole lot swaying and creaking as you walked across, conscious that there were only a dozen or so thin cables between you and a fifty-foot drop into the stalls. Sometimes there were no overhead cable fixings, so we had to erect fifty-foot, aluminium towers – again a tricky exercise on the slopes and steps of the old auditorium, again giving a feeling of being on the high wire in a circus. Not a job for the faint hearted - or sufferers of vertigo.

Towards the end of each contract, as the new carpets were going down, Old Harry would drive up from Bermondsey with the re-upholstered seats, all to be bolted down in pre-marked rows. Then with all the building work almost complete, the sound-system specialists and projection-screen erectors came in. These specialists each had their own target dates at various venues throughout the country. They couldn't be rescheduled, so everything had to be ready for them, or the completion date would be jeopardised.

Finally, as part of the re-vamping of the cinema image, on the re-opening night a screen or TV star or stars would be invited to cut the ribbon and address the crowds. As these often had to be booked a year in advance, again there was no way the opening date could not be met. So once the contract programme had been agreed, apart from earthquake or nuclear war, there was absolutely no leeway - no extensions of time – no reason at all for the contract not to finish on time.

So, to go back to our beginning, it was why on this particular night Alan was tearing his hair out, waiting for the last colour swatches to complete the job on time from the Old Man - who apparently was still in a tetchy mood.

Just as we were all despairing, his car drew up outside and he breezed into the auditorium, producing a schedule of paint and laminates' colours for the foyer. He'd already ordered the wall coverings from Muraspec, he said. Alan stubbed out his umpteenth cigarette with a sigh of relief. Crisis over. The decorators wouldn't walk off site and it was all go.

Dear Rachel. We loved her. She must have sorted out something for the following night. So we all relaxed and it was time to start thinking of the next job – somewhere in Newcastle, it seemed.

ALL TANKED UP

Spare a thought that when filling up your car at a service station, you are standing just a few feet above 3,000 gallons or more of highly inflammable petrol, with a network of fuel-filled pipes even closer. Not that this is meant to create panic – just that if it went up, you would be propelled into orbit as least as efficiently as the space shuttle – though the return to earth might be a little more bumpy.

The fact that this potential hazard isn't, is down to the men who put it all in place. And it was while engaged in this field of work, that I made the acquaintance of Mick and his gang.

Was it Oscar Wilde who once said that experience is the name everyone gives to their mistakes? Well, if experience had made Mick so confident, I was just glad that he'd made his elsewhere - and long before I met him.

In the Seventies, I was a new project manager in a company that specialised in refurbishment of service stations. All the large oil companies, BP, Shell, Texaco, Gulf etc., were remodelling their old style open-to-the-sky forecourts with their pump attendants, to create self-service pumps, under colourful canopies. One by one, they were being modernised with secure-till kiosks and miniature supermarkets tacked on. And with the rapid growth of car ownership and road haulage, their re-fuelling capacities were being increased with larger storage tanks and high-speed, digital-electronic pumps.

To bury a 3000-gallon tank at the correct level and

with the requisite concrete safety surround, the first requirement is a huge pit – much larger than the tank. Often, it takes up the entire forecourt area. So, much to the disturbance and annoyance of the neighbours, before anything can begin, the old concrete and tarmac has to be broken up using an arrow-breaker, a noisy, hydraulic chisel attached to a JCB excavator.

Following this, the old tank has to be removed, involving a complicated procedure of pumping out the bottom dregs of the tank and half-filling it with water, then pumping it out empty again for a crane to lift it away safely. And all this, before the new pit could be excavated.

For safety reasons, the top of the new tank has to have a metre of concrete between it and the forecourt slab, requiring a pit fifteen feet deep or more. As most old service stations were on made-up ground or, as in the London and Thames Valley, on unstable soft clay, digging the new pit had to be done carefully and the sides shored up with steel trench-sheets and hefty supports. Setting the new steel tank in place and surrounding it with concrete also had to be carried in a safe, specific sequence too.

Prior to meeting Mick and his gang, I'd worked with Eric, a long-standing foreman on the company staff. He always put the tank in by the book, carefully inserting steel trench-sheets around the perimeter of the pit, neatly held back by heavy timbers and struts as the digging progressed.

'Got me deals in,' he would announce when I drove in, standing proudly by a pit all neat and squared up, like an artist showing off his latest work. The younger foremen preferred using steel beams to hold back the sheets, but Eric was one of the old school and still used 'deals' – long, heavy timber baulks. Steel, trench sheets in lieu of the old timber 'waling' boards were as far as he would go.

Once the sides of the pit were securely restrained, he cast the concrete base and embedded heavy cable shackles into it, then allowed another day to let the concrete harden off. Finally the tank was delivered, offloaded with a mobile crane and carefully set down on the concrete. Cables were then attached to the shackles and passed over the tank, and tightened-up to prevent the tank rising up through flotation when new concrete was poured around it. As an added measure, he half-filled the tank with water to make it heavier. Luckily, there was usually a fire hydrant nearby to take a two-inch pipe. If there wasn't, for a small consideration, the fire-brigade would oblige – they were as interested as anyone to avoid a future conflagration.

Once the tank was secured and weighted down and Eric checked that all was as he wanted, in came the concrete lorries and poured concrete around the tank – but not too quickly – allowing the first couple of feet to go off a little and grip the sides of the tank, conscious of the ever-present fear that the tank might still float up and break the cables. If it did rise up even a few inches, there wouldn't be enough concrete cover over it and the local Petroleum Officer – whose word, like that of the Building Inspector was God in these matters – would condemn it. And if he did, whatever the cost, the whole thing would have to be dug out and started all over again, probably requiring a new tank. Otherwise there would be an empty tank and concrete taking up all that space for eternity.

As the rest of the concrete was poured in and the level rose, to ensure that the sides of the pit wouldn't fall in, Eric carefully released the trench-sheets around the sides one by one, his men pulling them up a little at a time, and then finally take them out altogether. With the concrete surround completed, he cast top slab, leaving a small square opening around the flange for connecting the pipes to the petrol pumps, together with the control cabling.

This completed, a specialist, petrol company contractor came in to connect up new fuel pipes to the pump islands, and the vent pipes to the rear of the site, as well as conduits across the forecourt area for the electrical services to the pumps and the kiosk.

The next stage was forming the petrol-pump islands, the payment kiosk and foundation blocks for the canopy and finally laying the concrete forecourt slab. Then another specialist gang would come in and erect the canopy - each oil company having their own design for the canopies, some preferring one overall structure, others, individual 'mushrooms', and so on

Following this, the petrol pump installers came on site, fixing them onto the islands and connecting up the electrics and fuel pipe runs. During this time, the sales' kiosk and shop would be fitted out and signage erected.

The very last stage before handing over the service station to the client was that of calibrating the pumps - to ensure that they delivered the exact number of gallons as shown on the dials. This was always carried out by government Weights and Measures specialists, carefully filling beautifully shaped, shining copper measuring cans, to check that the gallons coming out of the nozzle corresponded with the pump dial readings.

It so happened that during those years, the Seventies and Eighties, the whole construction industry was in a state of transition. Instead of building companies having a core labour force of directly employed craftsmen and apprentices, all the on-site activities - apart from the management - were being farmed out to specialist sub-contractors on a fixed price. Provided this was cheaper than the main contract price from the client, it took the risk out of making a profit. It did however create other problems, primarily in terms of quality control of the work, and keeping to programme – both of which was my job to plan and monitor.

Wherever the garage, the first and main task therefore, was to excavate the deep pit and install the huge storage tank. This operation took many days and was obviously expensive and time consuming. Which was exactly what Mick and his sub-contracted gang thought too, when I first met him on a service station refurbishment, just north of London. And having seen it done so correctly and safely with Eric, I was about to experience a shock to my system.

Mick had accepted the complete tank installation and forecourt work on a price. He was his own site foreman and would have none of 'all that palaver,' as he put it. Trench sheets and supports, shackles and cables, etc., were time consuming and costly, taking money off their 'bottom line'. There was also more than a touch of the macho approach in their method of working: groundworks were a challenge to be met with brute force and know-how, and then away to the next job.

Having been spoiled by Eric and his methodical ways,

all I could do was to watch as they proceeded – and hold my breath. Putting in the tank Mick's way required absolute self-confidence and nerves of steel. At times, it left mine shredded. Praying wouldn't have helped either of us.

My first visit to his site came just as the tank had been delivered. It sat on a low-loader truck, and already the huge crane was setting up on its jacks. To my surprise – or rather shock – there was just a damn great hole in the clay that had been machine-dug the day before. No sheets, no steel support beams. Nothing. Those that I had ordered just lay in a neat pile on the far side of the site.

The huge pit had apparently been bottomed-out and levelled that morning and as I drove up, a Redimix lorry was already pouring in concrete for the base. Below, two men were shovelling and levelling the concrete – no trench sheets, no props – just relying on the clay to hold itself up long enough. Except that with clay, you never know. One minute it looks fine, the next a huge chunk has sheared off and fallen in.

I had been reassured by the company's director that Mick's gang had successfully put in tanks to a few stations previously, without any mishap. What I also knew was that Mick and he were drinking buddies. So although I was concerned, on both accounts I felt in no position to commence my carer with the company in a confrontation. Plus which, Mick was a big guy.

As I walked across from my car, staring at this gigantic hole in the ground with not a single support, my face must have said it all.

'No worry, lad,' smiled Mick, flicking his wrist. 'We've

done this more times than you've had hot dinners.' And, having mentioned dinners, as soon as the concrete base had been poured and levelled out, the whole gang repaired to the local pub to let it set.

'To prepare for the afternoon,' smiled Pat, one of the gang.

After a few jars of Guinness for lunch, the boys felt it was time to go. I made do with just a half of bitter-shandy – much to their scorn.

'I'm driving,' I offered as an excuse, but it didn't seem to convince. Either way, I wanted to have all my wits about me if anything went wrong. Though if it did, what could I do? No shoring, no shackles, no cables... Already I could see the tank bobbing up like a cork on a sea of concrete. Sure. At their own cost they would have to dig it all out immediately and do it all over again. But what a disgrace – how to explain it to the oil company's management when they heard? And like it or not, this was now *my* contract.

Talking of lunchtime, bear in mind that all this was happening before the new Health & Safety Regulations began to bite in the Eighties, including banning all alcohol on site. Up to this time, not only the navvies but surveyors and managers too would often take a wet break at lunchtime with longs and shorts a-plenty. Now, quite rightly, anyone smelling of drink when booking in on site is sent packing, but at the time it wasn't even on the cards.

Well, that afternoon, as soon as the men were back on site, the crane roared into life and slowly lifted the tank into the air. Gently it swung it over the pit, with Pat tugging on a guy line to keep it parallel to the pit sides –

though more than once I thought that the tank was liable to swing him into it too. As the tank was being lowered onto the base however, it nudged the side of the pit at one end. With a squelch, a small section of clay sheared away and fell in.

With the tank still dangling half-way down on the crane, two men climbed down a ladder and started digging out the clay with two others hoisting it up bucketful by bucketful, until sufficient space was cleared for the concrete surround – still no shoring, no supports, *nothing*, the men standing in just the foot or so gap between the tank and the clay sides. I walked around the pit edge, anxiously searching for any more movement in the clay while at the same time wondering how far the nearest ambulance station was. It was a fine day. What if it started raining? Didn't bear thinking about.

Given Mick's connections with the boss, despite feeling distinctly uneasy I felt unable to challenge him without upsetting the applecart, and as I said, at the time, I was new to the company. Later in my career, I would have stepped in immediately to stop it - and I still have a conscience about having let all this happen at the time.

Well eventually the tank was set down on the concrete base, but still neither shackles nor cables to hold it down. It was crunch time. Was Mick really going to confound Archimedes and the laws of flotation? As if sensing that his new project manager might cause him problems, Mick had already sorted out the local fire brigade. They'd been waiting when we came back from lunch, and in a short time almost filled the tank with water to weight it down.

Half an hour later, the first mixer-lorry of the

afternoon drove up and began to pour in the concrete surround. But instead of pouring the concrete around the sides, Mick directed the spout onto the top of the tank. With the concrete-lorry drum turning very slowly, he soon had a heap of concrete all along the top, creating a huge additional weight on the tank – and a cubic metre of concrete weighs about two and half tons. He'd also ordered a quite stiff, low-slump mix. It came out like a morning's porridge from an afternoon sporran.

Slowly the pile mounted higher – must have been nearly two cubic metres of concrete - that's about five ton's weight, all bearing down on the tank. Very gradually, small amounts slid down the sides. With the time lag, it had half set by the time it began to build up at the bottom, but that wasn't that important. The concrete wasn't there for structural strength, but merely as a mass surround for safety and against corrosion.

All this was in the days before compulsory Health & Safety Risk-Assessments and Method Statements. This was the Mick-statement method. But would it work? What would happen if too much slid off the top in one go? Or if the tank did rise? Mick though, like Eric, was a specialist – but in his own way. Much as I feared the consequences if something went wrong, it was like watching an artist at work. He seemed to know exactly how much concrete to add to the top and how much to let slide down and fill the sides. As soon as one end piled up, he directed the spout at the other end and added to the heap there.

The rest of the gang of five kept watch, acting on Mick's gruff comments and directing the concrete flow, keeping the heaps piled up on top and all the while walking round and watching the concrete rise in the pit below, very lightly prodding it with long timbers to compact it as it rose – and all the time looking completely at ease. As he'd said: more times than I'd had hot dinners.

Slowly the pit filled and eventually the concrete began to come up over the top curvature of the tank. The worst was over. And despite his ostensibly cavalier attitude, I couldn't help noticing that for the top, covering slab, Mick had taken no chances. He'd ordered the full-specification strength and slump concrete mix.

So that was the trick, I thought as I began to relax. My hands though had been so tightly clenched that the palms were pitted with fingernail dents almost to breaking the skin. Had it ever failed, I wondered? The gang had also been contracted to work on my next service station renewal, somewhere near Birmingham. I wondered how many more like this I could take and still keep my sanity.

Eventually, the concrete was topped out and the last lorry drove away. The crane had long left the site, so if anything had gone wrong, nothing could have been done anyway. That's what one calls confidence, I supposed.

As I stood there, contemplating, Mick came over and slapped me on the back.

'Don't look so worried lad,' he smiled. I was older than him but I knew he was measuring age by experience. 'Never had one float up yet, y'know.' More than likely, I was thinking, it would be just my luck when it did.

It was six o'clock by the time they'd cleaned up, and as they piled into their Transit and took off, in the dead silence that seems to descend after any major building operation, I went over to look, just to make sure that the tank was still well below the ground level. It was.

Archimedes would indeed have been flummoxed.

The next day I drove out again, this time with a dumpy level. Loads of hardcore were already being dumped for the forecourt slab while the JCB was filling it around the pit and levelling it across the whole forecourt. With Jerry, one of Mick's gang holding the staff, I took the levels of the tank top and the surrounding ground, made some calculations, then quietly called Mick over to one side.

'The tank's a bit high,' I said softly.

'Can't be,' he grunted. 'Never is.' He glanced at the level's sketch I'd made in my Dims' book, then at me. 'How much?' he grunted. I showed him the figures. At first it looked like catastrophe. The forecourt level had already been set, but the tank had to have a full metre of concrete over, so we couldn't Kango-hammer any of it off to reduce it.

'About six inches,' I murmured, almost afraid to confirm. He squinted and looked across the site, then back to the figures again.

'Bastard must have moved a bit,' he grunted, then after a moment's thought said, 'Well. Only one thing for it. Have to raise the forecourt slab level a bit.' He looked across to the tipper lorry. 'I'll order a few more loads of hardcore for tomorrow.'

But it wasn't that simple. The kiosk floor-level had already been set and the slab by the pumps had to be dead level. To make matters worse, there was only a short distance to the road. Carefully, we plotted all the levels again. There was only one solution: to raise the whole slab and leave only a shallow step-up into the kiosk, which luckily would be under the new canopy and so protected from the rain. The awkward bit was that we had to form a steeper slope up from the road. Above all, we had to keep *shtum*. All of us. And it worked.

The next day, concrete arrived for the whole forecourt slab. Jerry, fresh faced and bright ginger hair, was the forecourt finishes specialist. When you are next filling up in a garage, cast a glance at that slab beneath your feet. If it's finished off like he always did, the surface will be neatly finished with light brush strokes and the joints between the bays will be straight and even with smooth-trowelled margins along the edges. Like Eric, he too was an artist. If he'd misjudged the setting of the concrete when he'd brushed it, bay by bay he would wait and do it all over again. And in case it rained, he had tarpaulins and boards ready to protect it as he went. But when it came to setting in the tank and covering it up, he was just as a gung-ho as the rest.

Not long after, I drove in to that same service station one day to fill up on my way to the Midlands. Yes, the incline up to the pumps from the road was indeed a bit sharp and the pump step up to the kiosk was pretty shallow, but it hardly noticed. And as I drove out, I smiled to myself; motorists must think it was like that on purpose.

I must have built about four more dozen service stations with Mick and his gang, and we never had another problem, though at the time there were nights when I lost sleep. Then came the Yom Kippur war, and with the subsequent oil price hike by Sheikh Yamani, the oil companies put everything on hold. Having put most of its eggs in the Service Stations' basket, the firm went into liquidation. Still, some of Mick's luck must have rubbed off on me. Just a month previously, I'd already decided to move on to another company anyway.

Now, from time to time, when I drive into a service station, I still see that yawning pit, the concrete slowly dribbling down the sides of the tank and the boys – full of Guinness - calmly making it all happen.

KICKING THE HABIT

Geoff, the bricklaying subcontractor, came into the site hut to look at some drawings while I was visiting the site one morning. The contract was an involved, external refurbishment project on a huge, Victorian redbrick block of flats in Kensington: slate roofing, window repairs, ornate brick and stonework replacements, washing down and external decorations. The whole building had been surrounded in plastic-sheeted scaffolding and covered with a temporary corrugated-iron roof to enable the work to progress in all weathers – and, it being Kensington, to satisfy the neighbours.

Geoff ran about half-a-dozen 'trowels', as we say for bricklayers, as well as his own labourers. They were doing a wonderful job with replacing and matching the flaking and cracked listed features such as cills, cornices and brickwork – artistry it was. When the scaffold came down, the façade would look as good as Victoria might have seen it.

Geoff was short and stocky with a shock of fair hair which, defying all attempts to comb it, he kept clipped very short. 'Wire brush,' the men teased him. Geoff was a serious type, didn't joke much, rarely went to have a drink with them at lunchtime – and was a marvellous, skilled brickie himself.

Whenever the men had a problem with dimensions, or turning a corner or keeping the bond, Geoff would come and sort it out in no time. Standing back and looking at the work, then glancing at the drawing, he would give instructions. And when he said it couldn't be done as the architects had drawn or dimensioned, we didn't question.

Just phoned them up and inevitably they agreed and issued an instruction to change it.

That morning, as usual, Geoff nodded when we met in the site hut, and after we'd clarified a detail or two and checked progress together with Jim, the site agent, I handed him the sealed envelope. He nodded again, a brief smile, and went out. He was going to bank the cheque straight away, in time to pick up his wife to go to their weekly meeting. No one else knew and I always handed him his cheque personally rather than leave it with Jim.

It had all come to light some four months previously. We all knew even then that Geoff had a habit. He would disappear for half an hour at most lunchtimes, but we never probed. After all, most of the men had a flutter now and then. Unlike Nobby, who'd seemed to take his losses with a kind of stoicism, Geoff couldn't hide the anxious expression he wore most times when he returned from visiting the nearest betting shop. Still, it was his business and it never affected his work – or so we thought. So I was caught on the hop one day when he came over to my car late one morning, just as I was about to drive off the site.

'Need to speak to you in private,' he said, his normally ruddy face, pale and tense. I glanced at my watch. I'd only called in to drop off some revised drawings on my way to another site. Geoff sensed my hurry. 'I know you're pushed, Dave,' he muttered, touching my shoulder, 'but it's got to be now. Please.' It was obviously something very urgent so I invited him into the car and we drove round to the next street.

'So,' I smiled as we pulled up and parked under a

railway bridge. 'Robbed a bank?'

'Not joking, Dave,' he said, his face taut. 'It's something real serious.' Then, after a short paused he added, 'I've just lost a packet of money. Betting shop.'

'Well,' I said, still smiling and trying to make him feel at ease, 'you must be used to it by now, Geoff.'

'No, you don't understand,' he said, looking straight into my eyes. 'This time it's the men's weekly wages. I've just blown 'em. All of it!'

Geoff always received a cheque from the company on the Wednesday, cashed it at his bank, then made up the men's individual envelopes of cash at home – his wife doing much of the donkey-work in the evening – to give out to them on the Thursday.

I couldn't believe what he was telling me. It would be over three and a half thousand pounds. And that was a lot of money in the Eighties.

'What? The whole lot?'

He nodded and looked ahead through the windscreen.

'Uhuh. The whole bloody lot!'

It was already Thursday lunchtime and in those days the men were paid in cash. Many had never used a bank account and preferred it that way – some for tax reasons, others because it gave them the freedom to short-change the wife with a long visit to the local on the way home.

'Look.' I said. 'The boys know that you often nip round to the 'shop' at lunchtime. But I never imagined it was that bad.'

Geoff looked up. I was sure those were tears in his eyes.

'Dave,' he murmured, 'you don't know the half of it,'

and in a low monotone he carried on. 'It was like this. I always used to gamble a bit. Never thought much to it. Most of the men place a bet now and then. But with me, it was more and more often. Soon, every day I had to place some bets somewhere – horses, dogs, football draws, you name it. I've tried 'em all, and each time thinking: "This one will do the trick." Of course, usually it didn't. But I couldn't accept that it was becoming compulsive. Just thought I could have a good time – and if a big win came in – well, the wife and I could have a longer holiday like, somewhere in the Canaries.'

He paused and looked at me again.

'You see. The more you start to lose, the more you think "Hey. Next time is my real winner," and you place an even bigger bet to try and get it all back.' He then proceeded to tell me how it had become an real addiction – that every time he passed a betting shop he just had to go in and make a bet. How he'd sworn to stop whenever there was a losing streak. But found he couldn't.

Suddenly he sat back and his voice strengthened.

'But up till now, y'know, the blokes' money has been like, sacred. I kept their wage packets in a separate large envelope. Never opened it till I got to the site and handed them out.'

'So how come this time?' I asked.

'Dunno,' he said, looking bashful, like a little boy. 'Yesterday, I just stopped off at the shop round the corner. Bet a couple of trebles on the early races and missed the last winner by just one place!' I suddenly saw the excitement in his eyes as he was describing it. 'Yep. If it had come in first, I would have got nearly a thousand pounds, you know!'

Sure, I was thinking, like the bigger fish that got away.

'Anyway,' he continued, 'I thought it was my lucky day. It gets you like that, you know. So I broke open the envelope, took out one packet and put two hundred down on the next race. It flopped. Then I put a few hundred on again to try and win it back. Then again. And by the time I looked round – it had all gone. The whole bloody lot!' He looked at me again. 'That's what it's like, y'know. It's the compulsion.'

We just sat for a few minutes, neither of us saying a word. It was already half past one. I couldn't think of what was going to happen. Some of his men lived from hand to mouth, and without their weekly pay packet some probably wouldn't even have food in the house by the end of the week. I had visions of them battering him to death with a handful of Fletton bricks and burying him in the mud. There were some rough characters among those brickies' labourers.

'Look, Geoff,' I said eventually, 'I'm glad you told me about this. And I don't hold it against you. You and the lads are doing a fantastic job with the brickwork. Anything else is really not my business.' I laughed, as I added, 'If I delved into the habits of all the men on site…' He didn't let me finish the sentence.

'I'm not just telling you this for nothing,' he said sharply. 'I need your help. It's desperate!'

'Me? What can I do, Geoff? I think you need to go and sort yourself out.' I didn't dare mention the word therapy. In the building industry then, it had connotations of mental hospital, psychiatrists, 'looney bins' – Colney Hatch or Broadmoor.

'Look,' he said, 'I must get the lads' money back somehow. Today.' He looked sheepish again. 'I need your help to get a loan from the company.'

I thought for a moment. Yes, we had a five percent retention on his account, but that was needed as a safeguard to make sure he would come back to pick up any remedial work later. And on a contract this large, the architect was bound to find some snagging, so my surveyors wouldn't release any of that money. But I knew I had to do something, not only because his men were vital to the success of the project, but also because I had always felt that Geoff was a really genuine character.

I sat staring through the window too for a moment, feeling Geoff's eyes searching me. It was an uncomfortable feeling. If you've never been addicted to drink or drugs or gambling, it's difficult to put yourself in that position. But I knew I had to try and do something.

'Look,' I said, 'there's only one thing for it. I'll try and arrange a meeting with our director. But you'll have to tell him the whole story, Geoff. No flannelling. Everything. Just like you've told me.'

'Well, if I have to, I have to,' he said resignedly. 'But it must be this afternoon.' Miracles, I was thinking, take a bit longer.

I phoned through to the office. Nigel was in a meeting, said his secretary,

'Look, Helen. Tell him it's really urgent and put me through. Please.'

She recognised the tone and after a few seconds, his voice came down the line. Without going into details, I managed to convince him to give us half-an-hour. Three o'clock, he said.

We drove back to the site and I bowled into Jim's site office.

'There's been a cock-up with Geoff's cheque,' I lied calmly. 'We have to go to the office to sort it out. Will you tell Geoff's lads they may only get their money Friday.' And without waiting for questions, shot out. Jim would have to suffer a load of abuse from the men, but not being his fault it would end there. I'd owe him one – as he was certain to remind me one day...

Nigel was dictating a letter into his Dictaphone as I knocked and we came in. He stopped and looked up.

'Right,' he smiled, 'what's all the fuss about then?'

We sat down facing him and as I re-told the story, with Geoff filling in the details, his face grew more serious than I'd ever seen. When we had finished, he sat back thinking, silent for nearly a minute. Under his fair wavy hair, his round face always had a ruddy complexion. I knew he himself had a problem, too. Alcohol. Perhaps that was what made him more sympathetic.

'Look,' he said to Geoff eventually. 'Dave is always singing your praises about the work on site, so I'm sure he's in favour of the company assisting you. And as you've been working with us for a few contracts Geoff, I'd like to help.' He looked straight into Geoff's eyes. 'But I've never done this before – for anyone.' He leaned forward and raised one finger. 'And I'll do it just this once – and never again – but on one condition.'

I tensed and I felt Geoff stiffen beside me. I had no

idea what was coming – but I sensed afterwards that Geoff must have.

'On one condition,' Nigel repeated, slowly and deliberately, 'and that is that you join Gamblers Anonymous. This week.' He glanced at me. 'And Dave. I want you to bring me proof on Monday that Geoff has done just that. Okay?' I nodded and looked at Geoff. It wasn't particularly warm in Nigel's office, but he was sweating.

'What can I say?' said Geoff. 'Thank you, Mr. Collins. Thanks very much for helping me out. I know it's unusual and yes, I will. I promise.' He half smiled. 'You know, the wife once made me phone them, but I never followed it up. So I know where to go. And yes. I promise. I'll do it tomorrow.'

We went through to finance. Nigel had already phoned and Martin made out the cheque.

'Don't spend it all at once,' he quipped, not knowing the circumstances. Geoff and I smiled, as though it was just an advance on his next draw, and we hurried out before he could say more.

Geoff didn't dare come back to the site that same day. Instead, I drove over, weaving in and out of the traffic as I'd never done before – or since. It was already late Thursday afternoon and I arrived just as Geoff's men were preparing to go home – and waiting for their wage packets.

'Listen, lads,' I said as I bowled into the canteen hut, 'there's been an office cock-up with a few of the sub-contract payments, and Geoff's is one of them.' And assured them it would be sorted the next day. They weren't at all happy, but had to accept the explanation, and I drove away praying that Geoff wouldn't have a relapse the next morning on his way in with the cash.

He didn't. That night he'd told his wife the whole story and the next morning he cashed the cheque and made up the envelopes. She came with him in the car up to the site on Friday afternoon, he gave the large envelope with packets to Jim, and immediately they drove off again.

'Got to see her sick father,' Jim told the men. They didn't question and were just relieved, as each tucked the small brown envelope into his pocket.'

'Wife has to come too,' he told me a few weeks later in the local cafe. 'Gamblers Anonymous' say it only succeeds if all the family does it. So we both have to go every week.' Then as we sipped the tea, he leaned across the table, adding quietly, 'because it hasn't gone, you know. It never goes, Dave.' He leaned forward. 'Listen. Every time I pass a betting shop, it's like a bloody magnet and I've got to force myself to pass by. It's like a real drug habit. And it's painful – a real pain in my guts each time,' he said, his face contorting 'because you're never cured. You've got to accept that you're always gonna have the urge. That you can never kick it. Only keep it under control. And it's only by keeping up the meetings and being straight with your family that you're gonna manage.' He wiped his hand across his forehead. 'And I'll tell you, Dave. Even after all that happened, it ain't easy. No. An' it still bloody well hurts.'

I moved companies shortly after completing that contract. We lost touch and we've never met again. But that encounter with Geoff taught me a lot. That in the hurly-burly of construction, with everyone chasing programmes and deadlines whilst trying to keep costs down, there is always the danger of losing sight of the person – the human being.

Geoff taught me that despite arguments over programmes and performance and disputes over money, I should remember that behind every subbie and every worker there's a living human being with his own family and problems. And that we should never forget that. And I haven't...

JUST A ROOKIE

From my very first brush with the construction industry – which came purely by chance – I discovered that the building game is full of larger-than-life characters. And Old Bob was the first I encountered when, as a student, I took a temporary building-site job – Bob and his story of Lisa Lotte. He was also responsible for my first 'wind-up' experience.

Bob was an old-time bricklayer, short and wiry with a face like tanned leather. He was much older that the rest of the gang and had been through WW2, from long before D-Day, to the final victory. What was unusual, however, was that Bob was a staunch Communist Party member – and for a country builder that must have been exceptional.

At morning tea, we would sit around the comforting warmth of a coke devil in the site canteen hut, one by one toasting our sandwiches over the glowing coke using a length of bent wire in one hand, while holding mugs of steaming tea strong enough to take the lining off your stomach in the other. It was my first experience of rough-toasted cheese sandwiches – and they have never tasted better since.

As we were half-listening to Jim, one of the other brickies, reading out choice items from the *Daily Mirror,* Bob waved his mug in the air.

'Just bloody comics, them papers,' he snapped 'Made to keep the workers happy in their ignorance, instead of dealing with the real problems,' then pulled *The Daily Worker* paper out of his back pocket.

'Who you gonna vote for then, Bob?' Jim chivvied him,

'Joe Stalin?'

Bob just shrugged, took a swig of tea and munched his sandwich. Much as the men teased him about his views – and his old, black seaman's cap, though he'd never been to sea – they deferred to him. He was a craftsman bricklayer that none of them could equal. When it came to an awkward quoin or setting out a bond, he was the final arbiter. In addition, they respected him because Bob read books. Real books. History, biographies – and, of course, politics.

I had taken a year off studying and was staying with a group of friends in a large dilapidated communal house near Bedford. Blokes and girls, all together, long before the hippie communes of the Sixties. Sure – there was the odd liaison, but mostly we just all knew each other and it was an economical housing solution.

Most of us had hoped to find work on farms nearby, which would keep us out of a wasted two years in National Service. The local farmers, though, wanted permanent lads – someone who would become head stockman or top milker or a reliable tractor driver, not a here-today-and-gone-tomorrow Johnnie. So we ended up in all sorts of jobs – for the girls, usually a local factory or shop and for the boys, labouring on building sites.

After cycling around the area looking for work, I was taken on as a general labourer with a local contractor. He was building three pairs of semi-detached council houses – all in cavity brickwork and tiled roofs. Apart from the cement-mixer, there was no mechanical plant or hoists, so I also had to learn to be a hod-carrier, keeping the bricklayers topped with bricks and mortar, up on the scaffold.

Banding, pallets and electric hoists were still a long way into the future and the unloading was entirely by hand, brick by brick. John, the apprentice brickie, would stand by the guard rail on the working lift of the scaffold, and one by one I would throw the bricks up to him straight off the lorry. After a few loads, especially in the wet, I could have committed the perfect crime – the wet bricks had completely worn off all my fingerprint ridges, leaving the tips of my fingers completely smooth.

My thumbs, though, became really sore, so the scaffolder, Alan took pity on my student hands and cut neat rubber protectors from old inner tubes, one set for my hands and one for my thumbs. He also made a stumpy wooden bat with which I could throw the bricks right up to the top lift, from the stacks bricks on the ground. There were many, many thousands of bricks in those houses, and nearly every one of them passed through my hands – sometimes two or three times if they had been unloaded onto the roadside and had to be taken up in the hod.

Learning to use the hod – two-sided box on a long pole - was no joke. Loading eight bricks into the hod was the easy part. Taking them up the ladder on my shoulder with neither the hod, myself or both going 'ar-e over t-t'– as it is said - was more of a problem.

After loading the hod and balancing it on my shoulder, I would gingerly climb up to the scaffold lift, holding the hod-pole with one hand and gripping the ladder rungs with the other. More than once I nearly lost my balance, had to let go of the hod and the whole lot tipped over and crashed to the deck below.

Gradually, however, I became quite adept, balancing the loaded hod in the hollow of my shoulder, then nipping up the ladder with both hands, before unloading the bricks expertly on the scaffold boards in a neat pile. Mercifully, the brickies tolerated my learning curve with humour. Later I became even more confident and was managing to load and carry up twelve bricks like an old timer.

As well as the bricks, the hod was used to carry up the mortar. To prepare the mortar, I was given charge of a small cement mixer that started on petrol and switched to paraffin once it warmed up. Hour after hour with the mixer chugging away, I mixed half a bag of lime, twelve shovels of sand and a measure of water, then turned it all out onto a plywood banker-board set against a corrugated-tin upstand.

To allow the mortar to become cohesive and easy for the brickies to work with, the object was to mix up a few loads of lime-mortar each afternoon, tip it onto boards on one side of the mixer, then leave it to go off and 'cure' overnight. First thing next morning it was knocked up again in the mixer and tipped out onto a board on the other side. This way it become so cohesive that with a gentle swirl of the shovel I could make small 'swiss-rolls' of mortar one on top of the other in the hod, and they would hold together in one mass until deposited as a neat cow-pat on each brickies' spot-board. That was the plan.

On busy days, however, I sometimes had to use the fresh stuff straight out of the mixer. It didn't cling, and half would drip away down the back of my jacket like a melting glacier by the time I'd reached the working lift. Mostly though, I began to manage quite easily and even had time to sit for a few minutes and read a paper or that week's *Statesman & Nation.* Which was probably why the men decided to wind me up. And it was certainly old Bob who put them up it.

It was after one lunchtime when, as usual Jim was reading out a snippet from the *Mirror*, this time about the Russians trying to take over control of all Berlin.

'Don't blame 'em,' snapped Bob, never losing an opportunity to 'put us right'. 'Bloody war would never have happened if the West hadn't built up Hitler against 'em in the Thirties.'

'Well. If we lets 'em get Berlin,' said Ernie, 'they'll be comin' over here next. That's for sure. Look what 'appened to the Czechs' - alluding to the Communist takeover in Prague in the late 40's.

'Listen, boy. If it wasn't for the Red Army,' countered Bob, 'we would never even have won the bloody war.'

"Ere. Give over you two,' muttered Jim. 'Can't I read my paper in peace?'

I was new to the site and listened intrigued, but the others must have heard it all before.

Well that day, unloading two lorry loads of bricks had taken most of the morning, so I hadn't had time to knock up any advanced loads of mortar. And following that political argument in the hut, after lunch the men must have decided they needed some light relief. So I was surprised when, by mid-afternoon, I found myself having to take up all the mortar I'd just mixed that was usually reserved for the next morning.

As fast as I hodded it up and got my breath back, one of the brickies would lean over the guard rail and yell: 'Muck. More muck!' or 'Bricks! Where's them ruddy bricks!' And it carried on like that all afternoon, with the sweat pouring off me and the fresh mortar dripping down the back of my jacket. As soon as I thought I'd filled the spot boards and come down again, came the yell: 'Muck. More muck!' or 'Bricks!' I just couldn't understand it.

Nearing the end of the afternoon, my head was burning and I was getting really annoyed and indignant. They had never chased me like that before. But as I began to load the mixer yet again, I happened to glance up. And there were the three brickies, with Ernie the apprentice, and Alan, the scaffolder, all leaning over the guard-rail and grinning at me.

'Reckon we made you sweat a bit, lad, eh?' chuckled old Bob, adding, 'surprised you didn't cotton on sooner.' And they all laughed like mad. So did I. It was a wind-up and sure enough old Bob was behind it. But like the considerate character he was, he'd still left me half an hour to knock up one load of mortar to start the next day.

Christmas came and went and my time with the gang was coming to an end. I had received my call-up papers for National Service. And during my last week, Bob happened to show his softer side with a poignant story that I have always remembered.

As usual, at lunchtime Jim was reading out his snippets from the *Mirror*. This one happened to be about the "No Fraternisation" policy for our troops in Germany being lifted.

"Bout time,' snorted Bob. 'Stupid regulation anyway!'

After the German surrender in '45, like many others, he had been kept on in the army of occupation, waiting his turn for demobilisation.

'We weren't allowed to speak to the Jerry civilians off duty,' he said. '"No fraternisation with the enemy," was the regulation. An' if you did and were caught, you were on a fizzer.' He sipped his tea. 'Trouble was,' he continued, 'there wasn't much for us to do except hang around the barracks. Near Aachen we were. The town was a shambles and the locals were all organised into gangs clearing the rubble and starting to rebuild – women an' all. No,' he murmured, 'No fraternisation. Bloody stupid!'

He paused and looked around.

'Y'see, the Jerries was starving. Money wasn't worth anything. And the local girls kept walking by the camp, or standing by you when you went to town, desperate to give you anything – an' I mean anything, like – for a packet of fags or a bar of chocolate. And some of the boys risked it on the quiet. But if you were caught, then it was jankers and loss of pay. And officers were told to keep the rule strictly enforced.'

'Well, one day, my C.O. came into my signal's hut when there was no one else about. Captain he was. Couldn't have been more than about twenty-five. Suppose he came to me because I was one of the oldest there. "Bob," he says, his face as long as the Siegfried Line, "Bob. I've put Lisa Lotte up the spout." Lisa was a local teacher. She knew a bit of English and had a pass to work for us as interpreter. Long, blonde hair and really pretty. Lots of the boys fancied her, but were scared of getting caught. "No fraternisation now," he would smile if he caught one of the boys chatting to her too friendly-like. And now it was *him* who'd knocked her up!'

"What am I going to do, Bob," he says. "I've broken no fraternisation orders." Crikey. He was in a right state. You see, he wasn't in just for the war, like us. He'd signed on and aimed for a regular commission. But for breaking regulations, he'd be in serious trouble. Charged and probably demoted. Might even have got cashiered. An' he must have been knocking off with the girl for quite a while, we reckoned afterwards.'

We were all sitting around the coke fire in absolute silence, fascinated by the story, the only sound, that of the mixer churning about twenty yards away. Bob took out a cigarette paper and tobacco pouch and rolled himself another slim roll-up between his fingers.

'Well,' he continued, 'I thought for a minute, then said the first thing that came into my head. "Got to get her an abortion," I said. "She won't," he says. "She's a Catholic. What am I going to do Bob? And I'm not even allowed to marry her!" So I thinks again. "Well," I says, "only one thing for it. You got to get posted out of here and quick before anyone else twigs, or she goes and complains to Major Standish." "But I can't just leave her," he whines, an' he's almost crying. "She'll have a baby. I can't just leave her like that in all this chaos here". So I says to him, "Look, Mr. Evans." We'd already chucked the Captain this or that long before in private, "Look Mr Evans, you might even be court-martialled; made an example of. How would you live with her then? No civvy jobs out here for people like you. And she won't get permission to go to England. Not for a while yet, I reckon."'

Bob swigged at his tea and stared into the coke devil.

'God. What a state he was in. An' I felt like his father 'cos he was really a decent officer. We'd been together since he'd been a lieutenant, all the way from Caen. But he wouldn't get any sympathy from the high-ups, that was for sure. Y'see, the Jerries was still looked on as "the enemy".'

'Anyway, I looked him straight in the eyes. "Listen," I says, "It's your only way out. You gotta ask for a transfer. And I'll bet Major Standish will prefer that to having the embarrassment of one of his officers getting cashiered, and all the scandal in his battalion." But the poor bloke just kept on moaning, "I've put Lisa Lotte up the spout. I can't just leave her, Bob. I can't."

Bob suddenly stopped and gripped his mug in his hands, staring into the red glow as if picturing the scene.

'Well. What happened in the end?' asked Ernie. Bob looked up, then around our small circle.

'Huh. You won't believe this, but a week later our whole unit was transferred to Hanover. Two days we were given to wrap up and leave. An' I'll never forget those faces as we drove out. Hers – and his. She was standing by the gateway looking after us. Don't know which of 'em was crying more.' He paused and looked into the red glow again, his face sad as we all sat silent. 'Anyway, two weeks after that, I got sent back to Blighty for demob. So I never knew what happened in the end.' He paused and stared down into his mug. 'Poor cow, Lisa Lotte...'

At that moment Tom, the foreman, came in to get a refill of tea. He always took his back to his own hut.

'What's up then,' he smirked. 'Run out of bricks?'

We all jumped as if woken from a trance then stashed away our mugs and packs, and without a word, trooped out into the mud.

DOING A BANK JOB

In the mid-Nineties, our company became involved in a rolling modernisation programme for two of the major national banks.

Having embraced computerisation and established centralised call centres, the banks were now reorganising and modernising all their high street branches to suit. The next stage – in which thankfully we had no part – was to serve redundancy notices on half the staff. The final stage, again in which we had no part, came a few years later: closure of many local, small, unmodernised branches.

Never mind the old music hall refrain: 'Don't put your daughter on the stage Mrs. Worthington', putting her in the bank would be even more precarious now. And speaking of daughters will later bring us back to Steve, our site manager on one complicated bank contract.

These modernising and upgrading contracts, involved the complete re-organisation of the entire banking area in each branch. Most local banks were in pre or post WW1, Victorian or Thirties' buildings. Each comprised a small, public space in front of the counters and a large area at the rear for the numerous staff to man the tills, do all the paperwork and answering telephones, as well as a separate office for the manager and often for a deputy manager too. So whenever we moved into a branch to commence work, as well as tellers at the counters there were many staff members at desks in this larger area behind the screen.

With the new bank image however, all that was about

to change. The largest floor area would now be for the customers, including interview rooms and publicity stands. The much-reduced staff numbers would instead occupy a smaller open-plan, computerised area to the rear of the new style counters. Often the manager's office was removed too - a call centre somewhere in Milton Keynes or Middlesborough would handle any queries or give advice. In addition, very often there would no longer be an overall manager; instead different members of staff had charge of the various functions such as loans, or clients, or personnel, etc.

So, whenever we had completed a refurbishment of a bank branch, only half of the staff remained who, on top of their regular banking tasks, were expected to sell insurances, loans and mortgages as well. Posted on the staff notice board would be a weekly list of personal results to spur them onto greater heights or – *pour encourager les autres* of those lagging behind. The way was open for the later mis-selling of insurance, PPI and other commodities' scandals that later led to innumerable legal challenges, and with some banks having to reimburse large sums to many customers.

None of this of course directly concerned our contract. What did, though, was that the banks insisted on each branch remaining open and functioning throughout our building works. Every day closed was a day's business lost – and banks are in the business of moving money daily – lots of it. And since most bank branches consist of just one, large, ground floor hall full of staff and the public, unlike in most construction contracts, somehow we would have to work between and around them – and safely!

To resolve this, the main bank's project director and

architects provided us with floor-plan drawings showing a two, three or four phased programme. This detailed which areas of the bank would be converted, one by one, in sequence and when. It also delineated how to isolate our work areas from the staff by erecting safety screens and a dust proof hoarding. Where this hoarding faced the public areas it would also have to be decorated - and where it exposed the secure counter and tills' line, most importantly, reinforced with anti-burglar, steel mesh.

On paper it looked fine. Except that all the services; electrical, telephone, IT, heating, ventilation and alarms were spread throughout the branch, so whatever we did in one area would affect the others. A cable cut or pipe damaged in one part could completely immobilise another – or even the whole branch.

To complicate matters further, there was also a small, steel cabinet full of delicate electronics called the 'File Server', which controlled all the computer transactions of the bank. One misplaced blow with a hammer, or careless nudge on that small cabinet could shut down the entire branch for a day or more – as well as possibly losing much valuable data. To make matters worse, by Sodd's Law, invariably this delicate item was to be found in most awkward place, usually at the intersection of two or three of the new work areas.

Here I feel it essential to acquaint the reader with the two infallible laws governing the construction process: Murphy's Law and Sodd's Law.

Murphy's Law states that states if anything can go wrong, it will go wrong; Sodd's Law that postulates that if it does go wrong, it will be with the most possible serious outcome; a sub sub-section of this is the Law of Directional Gravitation: that any dropped tool or spare part inevitably falls to where it does the most damage or into the most awkward place for recovery.

But I digress...

The vital aspect of bank contract work is obviously the need to ensure utmost security at all time. To avoid obstructing the public entrance, our workmen always had to use the staff door at the rear of the building, either for taking out demolitions' rubbish or bringing in new materials. This often opened into a dingy mews or back street, which could provide perfect territory for a real 'bank job', and there is an apocryphal tale of a heist by just such an entry during a refurbishment. So whenever this back door had to be opened, our foreman would position one of the demolition men - or the heaviest carpenter - by the door, hammer in hand. We never had any trouble, but two of the banks we refurbished later had break-ins – with a suspicion by the police that one of the temporary labourers had provided inside knowledge on the new layout.

Prior to commencing the contract, we always held a meeting with all the bank staff to explain the work and the different phases, and to gently warn them of the noise and disruption. Even so, on arriving the morning following the start or completion of a phase in the programme, they would find themselves in completely new surroundings, often more cramped and probably wondering what was going on behind those screens - and despite our best efforts, justifiably fed up with the inevitable noise and dust from Kango hammers and percussion drills.

So, with the bank remaining in normal operation,

each phase commenced with the erection of the dust-proof and secure partition over a weekend or during one night's work, and re-routing the services, as well as providing temporary, safe walkways where necessary. Often the route to the staff toilets (or to the rear of the cash dispenser), ran right through the work area, so with heavy work was going on overhead or around the staff, a timber tunnel had to be specially constructed. In general, apart from general disruption, the most onerous part for the staff was their proximity to unavoidable noisy works and dust.

As each phase was completed - and often there were three or more phases, the staff would find themselves moved around like sheep into ever smaller 'holding pens' until all was ready for the final changeover.

The 'changeover' was the most critical part of the whole operation, involving the removal of the old wooden counters and the installation of the new ones. Since the counters and tills were vital to the bank continuing to function, this in turn posed some awkward problems.

Firstly, the old counters were usually of heavy mahogany, to which thick safety-glass screens had been added during the Seventies and Eighties when bank robbing became a popular pastime. Dismantling them was no simple operation. In addition, all had concealed alarms and telephone cables wired in and connected to the security systems.

Secondly, the counters were also an integral part of the bank's security barrier: on one side was the public, on the other a secure area for bank business and cash. But in the reorganisation of the banking-hall area, the location of counters was usually changed - often by a distance of many metres, and to a completely different alignment. To prepare for this, a new 'secure line' had to be constructed in advance of installing the new counters, all while the bank continued to trade as normal – often cutting right across the existing staff area, yet allowing business to continue as normal as possible – a logistics nightmare that we had to negotiate in each bank.

Another major problem was that we had to adhere precisely to the main bank's overall rolling programme for its very many branches throughout the country. Our own department had some fifteen and the parent company many more.

Now, much of the new equipment and materials, including everything required for the new counters etc., were bank specials, ordered from designated fabricators and couldn't be obtained elsewhere - as were the specialist-systems and operatives. They too were working to the main bank's nationwide programme and scheduled for a specific date at each branch. So once that date had been fixed, it had to be kept. For example if we were not ready the for the counters to be installed, the specialist shop-fitters would be engaged on other branches for the next few weekends and our whole programme would be imperilled and delayed - a costly business.

This was true also for all the various other systems' specialists like IT, telecoms, fire alarms, security equipment, ATM cash dispensers, etc. And since nearly everything installed was a 'bank special' item, it would be on a similar precisely scheduled delivery, so the site agent and I had to check the bank layout again and again, forus to get orders in on time and firm up delivery dates. If something was missed out or arrived too late, there was nowhere else we could obtain it, so again, the programme would go awry.

Well, after many months of hectic work and approaching the final phase, everything is geared to 'The Changeover'. Behind our temporary partitions, electrical, ventilation and cooling systems will have been reorganised, and miles of new cables for telecoms, IT, security, fire alarms etc., stretched everywhere in thick plaited bundles called 'structured cabling'. Meanwhile, desks and equipment will have been delivered, all ready for the new arrangement.

On the Friday evening of the changeover weekend, immediately after closing time the bank becomes an anthill: demolitions men dismantling and removing the old heavy counters and temporary partitions, carpenters putting final touches to the new, secure-counters' line with its reinforced, steel-mesh screen, electricians extending lighting and computer cabling to the final terminations, ceiling fixers completing suspended ceilings and floor tilers and carpet layers trying to complete the public areas where previously the staff or public couldn't be disturbed.

Then, on the Saturday morning when the specialist fitters arrive with the new counters, we hold our breath while they are positioned, hoping that they will fit, yet anxious whether the electric sockets are in the right positions and so on, until every part is finally set up and in place, for the next day.

Another nail-biting item was ensuring that the secure, staff-door specialists arrive to connect up the electronic mechanism to this heavy door in the new partition. This is the only way through from the public to the staff areas, and how most of the staff will gain regular access during the day, by keypad.

Following all this, during that same weekend, on the secure side, the new staff desks are positioned and connected up to computer terminals and telephones, remaining light fittings installed in the suspended ceiling and, if possible, carpet laying continued – though sometimes, through lack of time, the staff will have to suffer working on bare concrete or wooden floorboards until the following weekend. On the public side, though, the floor has to be completely vinyl-tiled and carpeted to a pre-designed scheme, the reception desk positioned and connected up and at least one of the interview rooms, decorated and ready for use.

There was unfortunately the odd occasion when the bank's specialist fitters came a week or so in advance to check on the counter positions, only to find that their drawings differed from the latest architect's revision, and frantic phone calls had to be made to their head office to re-programme the counters, or alter the secure-line apertures already in place. Thankfully this was a rare occurrence.

Despite the standardised, overall scheme, each branch had specific problems – and often, awkward ones. In one branch, the new staff area was behind an old shop-front window, which had to be replaced by bullet-proof glass for personnel security –a very heavy and more complicated operation than it sounds. In another, the bullion hoist, which takes many kilograms of coinage up and down from the strong room in the basement every few days, had to be renewed, so in the meantime, two of our operatives, hammers in hand, provided security while the cash was brought up the staircase manually, each day.

Occasionally, the new counter line had to remain in exactly the same position as the existing one, which created its own problems because the new secure line could not be built in advance nor the new tills' apertures pre-formed. So on top of everything else, during that critical weekend, a completely new secure partition had to be erected, including integral heavy-steel mesh and cabling, and decorated, immediately after removing the heavy old partitions, involving extra night work over the weekend. And in some branches, the entire, old shop-fronts had to be removed and new aluminium-framed plate-glass fitted – again involving security measures - and keeping a sharp lookout.

One final complication was the ATM cash machine, and occasionally there were two. Of this machine, most people only see the window with push buttons in the street and expect money to come out on request. In fact it is a large and very heavy piece of equipment, yet extremely delicate. Since it has to be moved and connected up to the security system in one go, the company and specialists associated with it have to be programmed well in advance. And if new ones are to be installed, the opening in the external wall and its concrete base – with fixing bolts cast in – must be ready for the critical date.

In some banks, the back of the existing ATM protruded into our work areas, so every few days, all work was suspended for an hour or so whilst two of the staff were carefully shepherded through plaster dust and debris to refill the thousands of notes required into the back end.

Finally, cleaning and dusting, usually by a specialist office-cleaning company completes the work and late on the Sunday evening, the site agent and I lock up and stagger home. So on the Monday morning, the public walk into a completely new bank, often with the decorators still lining some of the less vital walls and perhaps working on a second interview room, whilst the odd carpenter is hanging publicity signage in the windows – and we can relax.

Whatever the problems, however, there is no way that the bank cannot be ready, secure and open on nine o'clock on that Monday morning – and it always was.

For us, as main contractors, there was a procedural headache that added to our problems. The main bank in its wisdom had decided to run the whole project under the system of 'Independent Project Management'. Normally, the architect's practice that plans the design, also oversees the execution of contract through to completion. Despite our general reservations about architects' management abilities, it was an arrangement that provided continuity and one with which we were all familiar. Now, in an effort to control the budget, the bank had engaged an independent 'Project Management Practice' to oversee the running of the works.

Now Project management is a skill that demands knowledge and above all experience. But independent, experienced project managers are thin on the ground and usually already involved elsewhere. In the vacuum, and in order to obtain the work, Quantity Surveyors' practices jumped on the bandwagon, re-styling themselves as 'project managers'.

Now a quantity surveyor (called the QS) is essentially

a building-contract accountant. His speciality is quantifying work, costing it and managing the legal and financial side of the contract as a whole. Controlling budgets is their speciality, rather than co-ordinating work to complete a project on time. Now, having taken on this new function, most of the new project managers we encountered were either quantity surveyors or freelance management professionals with – to say the least - varying capabilities. Often they were engaged through agencies and eager to make their mark, but many were less competent than our site managers and sometimes confrontational to work with.

Having added this layer of management, the bank's headquarters, in a further cost-cutting exercise, had also decided to dispense with the architects that after the design stage. Now, possibly in a new building on a green-field site, this may have worked. But all these contracts were in existing buildings, many of them Victorian and all of them having been re-modelled at least once in their history. So despite surveys, there was often no way of knowing what we would hit when demolishing a wall or taking up a floor, or where the existing services actually ran instead of where they logically were expected to run.

Inevitably, we hit problems that required a re-design of this or that feature, or of a services' route, yet the new project manager wouldn't commit himself to any form of re-design, or agree the extra cost involved. The bank however, had only engaged the architect for initial design. So precious time and tempers were often lost before the bank agreed to pay for the architect to visit the site when required - but again only after agreement with the local project manager. It was a crazy system – dreamed up no doubt by cost controllers and quantity surveyors' practices...

On top of all this, 'the bank must be open the whole time' edict, sometimes created ridiculous situations. In one, we were supposed to break out the old, stone-faced entrance and concrete entrance floor to create a new disabled access ramp and steps, all while the bank continued trading. When we pointed out that with the supporting steelwork this would completely obstruct the entrance and was a full week's operation at the best, the temporary project manager tried to dismiss it. Fortunately, the bank's area manager understood the situation, and unusually, closed the branch for that week. In a quid-pro-quo for his intervention, we carried out many of the works to the public area concurrently and thus made up much of the time lost.

And so back to Steve; fresh-faced, willowy and smooth black hair, the site agent on one of our most awkward contracts, the conversion of a London suburban branch – and the daughter.

This bank had started life in one converted Victorian three-storey, semi-detached house with an attic, on the High Street. Sometime in the Thirties, the bank had bought the adjacent house and knocked through a few wide doorways to form a larger branch from the two houses. Now, to create the new large public area, the entire party wall between the two houses had to be removed, with permanent steelwork support to the upper floors. This involved temporarily propping up practically the whole of the upper floors structure – and all whilst the bank continued trading.

We had allowed for this in our original estimate and provided a method statement to ensure that this could be carried out quite safely. When work commenced however and the special props and beams had been installed for the whole party wall to be demolished, the staff working on the floors above took fright. They demanded to be transferred somewhere downstairs or they would cease work – giving the area manager a serious headache. Which was why he didn't need another one from Steve.

Steve was one of a new breed of site managers, finished technical college, done very well and was intent on working his way up the management ladder. When we met on site at the outset, I could see that he already had the project sorted in his mind and exuded confidence. He joked that when he told his mates down the pub that he was going to do 'a bank job', immediately they asked form where he had obtained got the shotgun? Alas, such is the reputation of builders...

Now the men sometimes joked about Steve's irresistible chat-up lines, and 'extra-curricular' activities. What I didn't know however was that on this occasion, the particular lady in question was not only one of the regular bank staff, but was already engaged to be married. Apparently a 'friend' told someone, who'd told someone, until it reached the ears of her other half. The upshot was that he came storming into the bank one afternoon, fists at the ready, seeking redress from 'that bloody foreman!' Somehow, the lads prevented a punch-up by smuggling Steve out of the back door in time.

This led to an awkward meeting for me with the bank manager, and I had a real dilemma. The manager would have preferred my removing Steve from the contract but didn't feel he could demand it outright. I, in turn, didn't want to cause problems for the bank, which could prejudice other contracts. The job, though, was in a critical stage and, as on most projects, many on-site details were in the site agent's head and we were fast approaching the changeover weekend. To challenge Steve or not? That was the question. Personal matters are, after all, personal matters.

Thankfully, Steve got wind of what was happening. The following day, he called me round to the local café for a cup of tea. Bashfully, he admitted what had been going on with the lady but said it had been just a fling and was now all over. In addition, the lady cashier concerned was away on a course. But what when she returned? We couldn't have a repetition of a threatened punch-up in the banking hall.

Well, like I once said, one needs a bit of luck in this game. The following week, the bank hurriedly agreed to lady's request to be transferred to another branch – seemed that that was the agreement she'd made with her other half.

Either way it made Steve keep his head down and concentrate even more on the job. And to the relief of the main bank's area manager, we finished this difficult project on time and to everyone's satisfaction, and I moved onto the next one – thankfully less complicated - in Holborn.

DOWN IN THE DEEPS

Having been born under Cancer, a 'water' sign, the aqueous stuff should have been kind to me. Alas, throughout my construction career, water was to cause me no end of grief, either from above or - as on these contracts - from below.

Pete was a lanky six-footer. The first time I saw him, bent double in a trench, I couldn't imagine how he didn't end up completely tied in a knot – or ever manage to straighten out.

'Pete is never happier than when he's eight feet down a hole and half-way up his wellies in mud,' his previous contract manager told me, when he phoned to say that Pete would be available to be the foreman on my next job

'Look, Pete,' I said when we met at the start of the contract, 'we don't need you down below; the groundworks' sub-contractor will take care of that.' Pete just smiled. Behind the steel rimmed glasses perched on the end of his nose, were mischievous grey eyes that made you wonder what he'd got up to in his youth. I felt he would be doing what he wanted anyway. Not that I worried – as long as he managed the site properly and did the paperwork.

We had a contract to build a large Petrol Interceptor in the underground garage of Westminster tower block. By law, all car parks and garages must have these three-chambered manholes, which prevent oil and petrol from entering the main drains. Without such an arrangement, inflammable vapour could build up in the sewers and endanger the lives of the sewer-men. It might also cause an explosion at any time. In this case, the Council had decided that the existing one was too small - and anyway was partially clogged up and so required replacing anyway.

The garage was under a tall block of luxury flats in Victoria – not far from the Houses of Parliament. Having been designed only for private cars, it had very limited headroom, so any building operation needed to be done with some care. An added complication was that despite the heavy parking charges – or perhaps because of them – several media celebrities and millionaires used this car park to garage their cars - evidenced by the personalised number-plates on the new Rolls, Jaguars and Aston-Martins, as well as the vintage Bentleys and Morgans. One careless nudge by a JCB or dumper, or scratches from demolition debris, and we'd be in for a multi-thousand insurance claim – or more – and a lot of explaining to our managing director, when the press inevitably picked up the story.

Pete took this all in his stride. Totally unflappable. And for what we were to encounter lower down in the ground, I was glad he was: Running Water.

This new, concrete interceptor required quite a large pit: about six metres deep and as much along each side. After setting it out, the job started quite ordinarily. A specialist sub-contractor used an electric, laminated saw-blade machine to neatly cut a square opening in the thick concrete slab, then cut it up into pieces for disposal. The machine looked like a large, ugly, lawn mower and made noise like Concorde taking-off, but it did the job neatly. After that we could begin the deep excavation in the soil beneath using a JCB excavator –

and with the limited headroom, a careful operator. A small dumper took the spoil out to a heap by the roadside where, to avoid annoying Westminster council, it was taken away daily by grab lorry.

With Pete checking levels and dimensions, at first, all went well. But when the dig reached about five metres down, beneath the London clay we encountered sand and gravel. It was saturated and I suppose both Pete and I guessed what was coming, but preferred not to open our mouths to the devil, as it is said. Ground water.

Precisely because it is an unknown factor, ground water is the bugbear of all contractors. Even a survey borehole cannot always tell the whole story. If it was drilled during the summer and proved dry, the situation in winter could be completely different. If it missed old farmland, land-drains, when the excavation later cut across the ancient pipe runs, water would pour in from perhaps half a mile away. Above all, the simple borehole rarely distinguishes between a static water table and running water – often an underground stream, that would really cause a problem.

Well the JCB continued digging, and Pete and the groundworkers just carried on slipping in the steel trench-sheets around the sides of the pit and bracing them with timbers, Pete clambering up and down the ladder himself each time to inspect – and often to manhandle them as well. As his previous manager had said, Pete was never happier than when bent double in an excavation.

Progressively loosening the support timbers, he expertly supervised driving down the steel sheets, using the JCB bucket, as we dug deeper and deeper, but with every inch down, so the inflow of water increased.

Unperturbed, Pete started to use the two-inch pump he'd already ordered.

The borehole of the original engineer's survey had just shown possible water at five metres down – an understatement if ever there was one. At five and half metres, with the pump running continuously, the bottom of the pit was continually flooded. We had hit the groundworker's curse – running water – probably an old stream that ran down to the Thames, just half a mile away.

Pete, still unfazed, ordered a three-inch pump and when I drove into the site that day, there he was, bent double, prodding at the gravel to see from which direction the water was flowing and how to deal with it. The following day, there was a second three-inch pump but even the two running together continuously, were still struggling to cope with the inflow. Finally, when we reached formation level where we had to cast the concrete base-slab, the bottom of the pit was permanently submerged under a foot of water. And to fix the steel reinforcement and formwork and then pour the concrete base to the interceptor, we had to have a water-free pit.

Throughout all this, Pete was up and down into the excavation, probing and re-positioning the pump intakes, but to no avail. The task seemed hopeless. It seemed as though we were trying to drain the River Thames itself.

Unwinding his lanky frame from the pit, Pete climbed out, twitched his glasses and spread his hands.

'First time I've been beaten,' he murmured and we both knew it was time to call in the experts to deal with it.

The first Specialist Company invited wanted to use 'well-points'. These are perforated tubes, driven into the ground, from which a powerful mobile pump would extract the water faster than it flowed into the pit

'We'll drill about half a dozen, six-inch holes through the concrete slab around the perimeter into the ground and insert well-points,' the expert said. At least, that was the plan.

'And where will you pump the water to?' I asked.

'Well there's sure to be road drain outside somewhere nearby,' said the operative, confidently.'

I thought for a moment. On a new green-field site somewhere out in the country, there wouldn't be a problem, but in the middle of Westminster it would have to be into a road gulley. Apart from the fact that the nearest one was a hundred yards away, there would be an enormous flow of water. If the old road gullies couldn't take it, the resultant overflow would flood down the road into Parliament Square. It would hit the Press and the local Council would soon put a stop to it, and all the huge expense would have been for nothing. In addition, the powerful – and noisy - pump would have to run continuously day and night, a real problem in this smart residential area.

Meanwhile the days were passing, eating up our contract programme. I sent letters to the client explaining that we had hit running water – and advised them that since it was not mentioned in their survey or the contract documents, this would extend the programme and involve them in additional costs. Forewarned is forearmed. My declining the use of well-points though, still left the problem unresolved.

So we brought in a second specialist company.

They proposed a Bentonite injection technique. Bentonite is a very-fine, grey clay that comes in powder form from the American Mid-West. In water, it swells to many times its volume and forms an impervious, colloidal layer. It is a more expensive, but a one-off operation that is widely used in waterproofing large civil-engineering jobs. Would it do the trick here, we wondered?

'No problem,' said the specialist sub-contractor. 'We'll drill holes down to below the water level and inject a Bentonite slurry into the gravel all around your steel trench sheets as well as into the bottom of your pit. It will form something like a clay bath,' he explained, 'and you should have a pretty dry hole when you dig it out.' A distinct advantage was that it wasn't a noisy process.

The promise sounded too good and I could sense Pete's scepticism shining through his glasses. But we had to find a solution somehow. All we had was a huge, square, deep, paddling pool, in the middle of an expensive, underground car-park. This method wouldn't be cheap but luckily, since there was no mention of running water in the original tender survey, most of that cost would have to be borne by the client as 'extra to the contract'.

Well, all our own work stopped for the next week whilst they drilled down into through the concrete slab all around the pit and inserted their narrow steel tubes and into the into ground. Then a large, powerful pressure pump injected the Bentonite slurry down into the gravel. From time to time the pressure forced the slurry back above ground and splashed everyone and everything in a blue-grey slime – just missing the

Bentley, which luckily, along with other nearby cars, Pete had had the foresight to cover with plastic sheeting. Each day we prayed that none of the owners would come down to get their car from the garage. No one did and we supposed they were away on the Riviera or Bermuda – hoping they would stay there for a while.

Meanwhile, the pump throbbed and hissed and huffed, and the rubber connecting pipes trembled but we had no idea how much slurry was going down and if it was doing the job. We were totally in the hands of the experts who worked long hours, the pump thumping away and their overalls now completely covered in the grey muck. Finally, they shut down the pump, pronounced that they'd succeeded, coiled up all their pipes and departed with all their equipment. I could see that Pete was still a bit sceptical but it was our best chance.

Well, we started work again and the JCB began to dig out a gluey mixture of heavy grey Bentonite clay and gravel that incidentally now made driving the trench sheets much harder and slower. With the original programme already shot to pieces, we were now losing even more time but for a while, it looked as though we had won and soon we reached the formation level of the new concrete slab.

The underground river though hadn't given up. Through sheer pressure and force of running water, slowly it began to wash away some of the Bentonite, and seep into the pit again. Frantically, the men bottomed out the pit and managed to pour in a layer of concrete blinding, but still the water trickled in.

Pete went down the pit again, trying to stem the

leaks through the joints in the sheets but as fast as he stopped one, another seeped in and soon he and the men were ending up as splattered in grey mud as the specialists had been. And despite all their efforts, just as the steel fixers finished laying their mesh of reinforcement rods for the base slab, so the water began to rise again.

'Take more than a little Dutch boy and his finger to stop that lot,' shrugged Pete. 'I'll get the three-inch pump working again.' So digging a small sump-pit in one corner, he pushed the suction pipe down alongside the concrete blinding. At first the water did sink down but all pumps require a certain depth of water to suck, so every few minutes he had to wait for the water to rise again until there was sufficient for the pump to extract it.

'Up and down like a ruddy yo-yo,' muttered Pete. This was one hole he obviously wasn't going to enjoy.

When the client's engineer came, he noticed that the water was rising above the steel reinforcement mesh.

'Can't pour into that,' he muttered. 'We must have a dry pit before you pour the concrete.'

'Don't worry. We'll get the water down,' responded Pete. I admired his confidence.

'Look,' he said with a wink, after the man had gone, 'good concrete sets even under water. They do that every day in harbour jobs and dams with a dremel spout. I'll order a strong, stiff mix with extra cement. We just have to manage to pour it in during those few seconds when the pump sucks it down. And once it's down, it'll go off nicely – even under water.'

'Take your word for it,' I said. 'We don't want to have

to jack it all out again.'

'Leave it to me,' he smiled and with that same mischievous glint in his eyes as when we first met, added, 'best get a photograph for the engineer as proof though, eh?'

I knew we had no alternative. The longer we delayed pouring the slab, the more that underground stream would wash away the Bentonite and we'd be back to square one.

So, well after midnight that night, I drove to the deserted site, taking my camera and flash with me. With the pump still running and no one about – in that part of London, only the Call-girls are around at that time – in one of those few seconds that the pump sucked the water down, I snapped a few shots of the "completely dry pit". The next day, waiting for a similar 'dry' moment, Pete poured the concrete to the bottom and the first riser-section of wall, taking us to just above the water table level. And we prayed that the rich concrete mix, now held tightly between the shuttering and the steel trench sheets, would now set solid. And it did.

A few days later, at the next site meeting, the engineer looked surprised that we'd managed to pour the base and were shuttering the walls for the next concrete pour. Climbing down into the pit, he looked at the bottom. It was still damp but no more water was entering. It has worked.

As the man came up the ladder, looking a bit baffled, Pete pulled my photographs out of his shirt pocket.

'Thought you'd want proof,' he smiled. 'Dry as a bone, squire – give or take.' Even I was convinced. And after a few days, the pit was indeed completely dry and we could carry on and complete the job.

Pete had only been allocated to me for this contract, so once we'd handed over, he moved back to his previous manager – and I was sorry to lose him.

My 'underground water' problems though, were far from over.

We were in the final stages of a large, new school project in the Home Counties. The main building had been finished and internal fitting-out was almost complete. All we had to do now was to finish off the drainage.

Pat and Gary were down a deep shaft trying connect up our new main pipe to the council sewer. The foreman and most of the gang had already moved on to a new site, leaving just these two to complete the connection, which should have been a simple job.

As luck would have it, the main sewer ran down the middle of the only main road into the small country town. So to dig down, locate it and make the connection, we had to install temporary, one-way traffic lights on the busy road, creating log-jams during the morning and afternoon rush hours. This was obviously upsetting the locals and through motorists, and we were not the favourites of the month, so the quicker we could get it out of the way, the better.

As I visited that afternoon, Pat poked his head up out of the pit.

'Found the sewer pipe!' He shouted. He heaved out a shovel of clay and rested a moment. 'But we can't make the connection.'

'Why not?' I asked, peering down.

'Length of wood in the way. Stuck in fast.'

I looked down to where he was pointing. A long, wedge shaped piece of blackened timber rose out of the mud alongside the sewer. By Sodd's Law, it was directly in the way of our new pipe. 'Must have been left here when the old Victorian drain was put in,' Pat muttered. 'Stuck fast.'

I straightened up and looked around at the line of motorists waiting for the lights to change. It was rush hour. Apart from the local inconvenience, the costs were mounting rapidly. We'd already had the road up for two days trying to locate the sewer. With our drainage pipe already in and backfilled, there was just this last metre and the connection left to finish the job.

Without a second thought, I shouted back.

'Well, we have to get the wood out somehow. Won't be able to get the connection-collar on otherwise.'

Gary grabbed the end and tried to pull it out, but having been there for so long, the timber seemed in no hurry to come out.

'Won't budge,' shouted Pat. I wondered what was holding it? It must have been driven in deliberately and very firmly when the Victorians ran the sewer.

'Try rocking it,' I said. Gary started to rock it from side to side and heave at the same time. It was certainly stuck fast but slowly the wooden point began to rise from the bottom of the trench.

'Got the bastard,' shouted Gary as he finally pulled it out.

'Great,' I said optimistically, as Pat handed it up to me and I threw it onto the pavement. 'Now we can get on.'

If only. A second later, from the socket where the wood had been stuck, as surely if Moses had struck the trench bottom with his staff, a geyser of water shot up alongside the pipe and flooded into the pit. Gary stepped back, cursing as the water soaked his boots and trouser bottoms. Up till then, it had been a dry dig. Pat got drenched too and climbed out of the hole, his string of curses giving mild apoplexy an old lady who happened to be passing nearby.

After a few minutes, the miniature geyser subsided but it still left most of the pipe and the bottom of the trench under water – running water. Luckily, we had already cut open the side of the main sewer in preparation for the connection, so luckily the water had somewhere to run away.

'Spring!' Pat spat. 'A bloody natural spring. That's why they must have driven that wood spike in, in the first place!' Instinctively, I grabbed the timber and handed it back down to him. He drove it back tight with a hammer, and although it did reduce the flow, water continued to flood in.

'Just what we needed,' I muttered, glancing at the traffic piling up at the red-light end again.

To secure the pipe to the main drain, we had to place concrete around our new saddle-joint to the sewer, and there was no way we could do this in fast running water. And with this kind of flow spurting up alongside the pipe, even with a three-inch pump running continuously, ordinary concrete would be washed away as fast as we placed it. But we had to do something. And quickly.

'Prompt cement,' I shouted as Pat bent over double again to clear away the silt washed in by the spring.

'We'll have to try prompt cement. Get the pipes and collar ready for jointing. I'll drive to the builders' merchants right now.'

Prompt-setting cement powder hardens within seconds of being mixed, and seemed the only solution. If that didn't work, we'd have to dig out a large sump and bring in a much larger, motorised pump – and the road-up signs would go on and on.

I returned with two small sacks – it was expensive stuff – and handed one down. Pat promptly tore it open and spilled it around the joint. Immediately, it was washed away.

'No. Not like that,' I yelled. 'You take a handful and hold it by the joint until it goes off.' Disbelievingly, he clenched a fistful and held it to the pipe. When he let go, a small carbuncle remained stuck to the sewer.

'Right, Keep doing that, bit by bit. Bit by bit.' I called down. So, holding a fistful in place each time, Pat repeated the operation again and again until after a while, he looked up, his face pained.

'The water's f---in' cold and my hand's gone f---in' numb,' he muttered. 'I feel like that bleedin' Dutch kid pluggin' the dyke. And,' he added, 'there's no more cement.'

I handed down the second bag. We'd already been at it over half an hour.

'Have a rest,' I said. 'Let Gary have a go.'

Gary held a piece of sacking around what had already set but the young lad wasn't as capable and immediately, half of the bag was washed away again.

'We'll need two more sacks.' Pat shouted up. So off I drove to the merchants again.

"Ere. What you doing? Eatin' it for lunch?' the counter-hand smiled. 'And there's only two more bags left!' Being expensive they didn't keep a large stock and we were taking almost all of it. But it was no laughing matter. It was getting late and the thought of another day's costs and continued traffic chaos didn't bear thinking about.

Back in the road, I handed him another bag and Pat carried on doing his little-Dutch-boy thing again. Eventually, little by little he managed to build up sufficient set cement to cover and secure the joint around the saddle. But now, with nowhere to drain away the spring water began to rise in the bottom of the pit, soaking the man's boots again. Eventually, balancing on some lumps of clay, Gary managed to shovel pea-shingle over the joint then climbed out.

'B'Jeasus,' Pat gasped as he straightened up, 'never had anything like that. Ever.' Neither had I, I tried to console him. Pulling out the timber again, he flung it onto the pavement with a mighty oath – I was glad the old lady wasn't passing again, and he climbed out.

Still swearing, he started up the JCB and he and Gary began to back-fill the pit and pack it down. It was nearly dark by the time they laid the temporary tarmac and both the town and we were glad when we took the temporary lights away. That spring is probably still running down there alongside the pipe to this day.

The perils of water ingress continued to dog me throughout my career however – both from below, and later, from above too. So much for a favourable birth-sign...

TRADES UNION BLUES

It was a staunch, Trades Union acquaintance, who once told me that the trouble with middle-class liberals, was that they thought that all working-men were noble. The workers however know that there are villains among themselves too, including some of the organised ones. As we were to discover with a vengeance, when 'the Union Man' paid us a visit during one of my contracts.

The project was a new, huge garage-cum-tyre-store in Essex; heavy steelwork frame, corrugated-metal wall-cladding and smooth finished, concrete floor and at one side, a new, three-storey, office block.

The job had already been delayed by a month through having discovered the rubble of old houses, bombed and levelled during the war. These had to be grubbed out and the voids filled with lean-mix concrete. To compound matters, we were in one of the boom periods, and after the serious cutbacks in production facilities following the Three-Day-Week crisis of the Seventies, there were shortages of cement, concrete and bricks. Every builder was screaming down telephones at the suppliers.

This contract had commenced a month or so before, but was already in trouble when I took it over. The previous foreman, who was new to the company, had left suddenly under a cloud so there was a severe delay to the programme. All we had was a new, bare, steel frame and the foundations for the brick-built offices.

Charlie, tall and balding, our new foreman in charge had begun to get a grip on things, and after surveying the situation with him, we knew that we had to get that concrete floor down, which was the vital part of the contract programme. So in an effort to make up time, I decided to use a new super-fluidity additive to speed up casting the concrete floor.

The tried and tested method of pouring concrete floors is in large, alternate bays with finger-width joints between to allow for contraction when it sets, and for later expansion in areas under full sunlight. Our problem here was that even by pouring a few bays at a time, allowing for setting and then removing the formwork around each bay, it would be a slow process and further extend our programme even further.

After consulting the literature and speaking to Readymix concrete suppliers, I opted for this new, super-fluidity process. It is usually used in heavy beams and piers to allow the concrete to flow between congested reinforcement steel-bars that take up much of the space inside the formwork. I hoped that because it was self-levelling, using it here would allow large areas to be cast in one operation and so avoid the usual separate, small bays. It was a gamble, but time was now of the essence and I could see no reason why it should not work. As it is said: 'blessed are those that believe...' And after levelling the floor area and laying the hardcore, we set up taut, string lines to show the finished levels.

As it was a rapid process, to ensure continuity, by ten o'clock that morning we had a queue of concrete lorries along the main road outside the site, all waiting to come in and unload in and keep the operation flowing – literally.

To obtain the super-fluid concrete, as each concrete lorry came on site, measured amounts of the expensive liquid were added to the drum and allowed churn for a few minutes, then poured it out onto the floor. With this additive, the concrete mix came out of the drum like something the morning after an evening dose of Senna pods, and flowed like water.

By gently sending it on its way with prepared timber T-pieces, Adrian the ganger and Charlie, and two others, wellie boots on, kept it flowing and spreading up to the level of the string-lines all across the floor, all across the slab area. No shovelling, and no alternate bays and formwork with its time consuming, expansion joints. And to my great relief, it worked. By three o'clock, we had completed the whole garage area – over 200 square metres.

Luckily, the corrugated-sheeting, roof covering had already been installed, so there was no risk of a too-rapid drying out. Drying out? That was a joke. The whole month had been one glorious English summer – rain nearly every day.

To provide a hard, smooth surface, the floor had to have a power-floated finish. This involves a machine that looks like an upside-down propeller attached to a lawn mower and is a specialists' job, so we had engaged a recommended gang who had done this before. They happened to be based in Scotland and that same afternoon, came down with the equipment and personnel in a van and a car.

After walking round the site and prodding the concrete here and there, they all piled back into the car again.

'Hey. Aren't you going to float it?' I called out, anxious, as their foremen engaged gear.

'Concrete needs another few hours to go off,' he said. 'Won't be ready 'till tonight.' Then they disappeared.

I was a bit concerned their leaving site so soon, but having been recommended by the concrete company, I trusted that they knew what they were doing. It turned out they'd taken advantage of the run down south to go to a night-club in London. We admired their stamina – driving all the way down from up north, then power-floating a huge floor, all after a wild night on the town. Still. As long as they got it right. They were, after all, the specialists – and were on a price.

Well, we arranged night-time access and floodlighting, left one man on site and went home. They must have come back and started well after midnight, and when I drove in the next morning, they were just giving the final polish before setting off back up the M1. God knows what they did for sleep - but it was an excellent job. Now we could begin wall-cladding the steel frame to the main garage area.

In the meantime, we had continued building the brickwork office block. It had reached roof level and its flat roof was going ahead too. So, having come out of the dodgy ground and the mud, and with the concrete floor finished and work commenced on the customers' car park and approach road, we had pulled back at least two weeks of the programme delay and I was feeling more optimistic.

A few mornings later though, as I drove into the site, Charlie shot out of his hut and called me over.

'Man to see you,' he grimaced as I climbed out, adding quietly, 'looks like trouble.'

That usually meant the local building inspector having discovered something he didn't like. Not this time. The figure waiting inside the hut was heavily built man, bearing a reasonable resemblance to a younger

Kray Brother, but with a Lee Travolta hair-do and dressed a little too trendily for a council official.

'Who's in charge here,' he snapped.

'Well, I am I suppose,' I said, conscious that Charlie had ducked out of this one.

'How many men here are in the union?' he asked.

'Don't know,' I shrugged, knowing full well that none of them was. 'It's a personal matter. We don't ask.' Most of the men were in fact self-employed and on 714 sub-contractor certificates. Made their Income tax less painful they maintained.

'Well they've all got to be in the Union,' he snapped. 'You contractors are always using unorganised labour.'

If only he'd have known; he was barging into an open door. Unlike many of my colleagues, personally I wasn't against unions in principle. Yes, there were the jumped up wreckers like once in the Midlands car industry – though I could never understand how it is that despite militant Communist CGT-led unions, France has three successful car manufacturers, yet Leyland and Ford Dagenham went down the pan unable to negotiate with our much less extreme unions. Might it have been more one of management failure, rather than union militancy?

It is also true that prior to legal enforcement of the new Health and Safety legislation, unions often helped to ensure safety and decent welfare conditions, especially on very large projects. But in a small, transient site like this with less than twenty men at any time and with a company like ours, which provided decent site conditions anyway and had a strict safety policy, I didn't see the point.

'Look,' I said. 'You're quite welcome to go and ask

them yourself.'

'I have done,' he snapped. 'Went to those two over there. Told me to f--k off.' And pointing his finger at my chest, he continued, 'I want you to get them all together. Now.'

'Can't do that,' I said. 'They're busy and we've got a tight programme. But you can speak to them during the lunch break.'

'Are you telling me I can't speak to them now?' He leaned forward, wagging his finger. 'I can't hang about, y'know. And I've got a few other sites to visit.'

'Well, you are welcome to go round the whole site yourself,' I said, with my democratic principles being sorely tested and trying to keep calm, 'but you'll need a hard-hat.'

'Haven't got one with me,' he muttered. So hoping it would mollify him, I loaned him mine.

'Be our guest,' I said. 'Feel free.'

As he stomped off towards the brickies, I hurried into the hut and telephoned the office, praying that Old Les up on the scaffold, wouldn't tip a spot-board of mortar or bricks down on the man in the meantime.

Sam, my surveyor answered the phone. Sam had had a terrible year. His young wife had died with cancer and he'd been left with an infant son. Somehow, his sense of humour had helped him get through it and despite all, we usually started each phone call with an 'Inspector Cluzot' dialogue: *'Ave you a leesence for the moenkey..?'* etc.

This time, there was no joking and a string of expletives came in response, as I related what was happening. We agreed that I would play it by ear and do the best I could. Meanwhile he would alert our director.

I put the phone down just as the Union man clomped back into the office and slammed my hard-hat on the desk.

'Right,' he snapped, 'None of them are!' Is, I wanted to say, but didn't.

'Well I can't force them,' I said, wanting to add 'it's a free country', but didn't.

'Look,' he snapped. 'If they don't sign up, then I'll blacklist this site.' He wagged his finger again. 'The cement works and the concrete depots are unionised. As well as most of the brickworks. One 'phone call from me, and you'll get no deliveries. Nothing!'

He opened a brief case, took out a sheaf of membership forms and held them up.

'See these? I want a dozen members signed up from this site. And by the end of next week. Okay?' Then he took out his card and gave it to me. 'And it's got to be this union branch – not anyone else's. And to me personally, 'cos this is my patch!'

I glanced at the card: his name, area organiser, address etc. Obviously trying to make a reputation for himself with his head office. It was blackmail. Did they know what he was doing? And were others were doing similarly?

As he walked out of the site and up the road to the railway station, I found myself shaking with indignation. There was absolutely nothing about workers' solidarity in his manner or ambition. He was more the type who could have been a SA trooper in Nazi Germany or one of Stalin's minions. Perhaps this was the way Uncle Joe had started? The whole sorry business was testing my egalitarian principles.

I was even more annoyed at his intrusion, because the weekend before, we had overcome a major problem. And we never could have managed it without all the men co-operating and pulling together, over and above any legal or contractual requirements.

Commercial buildings like the office block we were building, are not designed for centuries and the client had apparently wanted the most economic – i.e. cheap – job. In response the architect had specified bog-standard, pre-felted chipboard for the boarding under the flat-roofing felt. Unfortunately, owing to the wet summer, even though it had been felted and weathered, with the windows not yet installed, the chipboard had absorbed so much moisture from the atmosphere, that it had been weakened. So when a plumber put his foot straight through the roof whilst dressing a flashing into a gutter, it was obvious that it had begun to loose much of its strength. The architect admitted his mistake in specifying it – a none-too-common occurrence, I might add, and instructed a stronger replacement boarding and new roof-felting.

Directly underneath, on the top floor however, all the services had already been installed, and the offices had just been plastered. There was no way we could we just remove the whole roof and risk everything getting soaked. This called for something special.

After speaking to the men and 'phoning around, and promising bonuses etc., etc., I managed to arrange for all the chippies and labourers to come in, together with roofing contractors, plumbers and scaffolders, for that weekend.

Starting at five on a damp – but luckily rainless – Saturday morning, in a pre-planned military operation, starting at one end of the flat roof, we stripped and removed the old felt and boarding, and screwed down new waterproof ply – no hammering allowed - which would have brought down the plastered ceilings beneath. As soon as the chippies had laid a section of the new roof-boarding, immediately the roofers followed on behind with new felting and then at the junctions, plumbers dressed the lead flashings to the office building brickwork.

There were about fifteen men on and around that roof, all working 'like the clapppers', as we say. And God must have smiled on us just that day; heavy cloud but not a drop of rain. By nightfall, we had stripped and weathered that entire flat roof with hardly a spot of damage to the offices below. It just left a few hours on the Sunday for the plumbers to put the final leadwork touches.

All the men had accepted the challenge and sure, they received overtime and a bonus, but they certainly hadn't done it only for the money. It was a professional pride in rising to the occasion and working together to resolve a crisis – to a common end. And isn't that what it's all about, union or no union?

Anyway, I doubted whether that obnoxious official would appreciate any of that, so on the Monday I told Charlie to call the men into the mess hut. Gently, I explained the situation – and the danger that the site would have to close the site down if he 'blacked' the supply chain. There was an alternative, I explained. Some of them would have to sign up to the union – just the once.

It was an uphill struggle. They were all self-employed and rank individualists. Wouldn't even agree to be directly employed – and not only for tax purposes. On top of which at least two were probably closer politically to the National Front, than to the Labour Party.

'Look,' I pleaded, 'all you have to do is sign the forms and make a one time payment. You don't have to go to meetings or anything like that.' With true English righteous indignation, a torrent of derision spiced with four lettered words came back at me. But it was no laughing matter. That official wouldn't give up and we could have the site completely neutralised if the boys didn't come round.

'Listen,' I pleaded, 'it's *your* jobs that are at stake if we can't get materials delivered.'

'So we'll go and work elsewhere,' was the response. At the time, there was a lot of work about.

We argued for another twenty minutes without getting anywhere.

'All right,' I said, growing desperate, 'just fill in your particulars and sign. I'll send in the forms and the company will pay the dues. Okay?'

The general mutterings didn't sound encouraging. With some it was a matter of principle, with others it was the fear of being on a union register. It was common knowledge that 'unofficially', a specialist agency held files on any militants and prominent union men, who were then blacklisted by the large companies when looking for work. A recent official public enquiry exposed a rotten saga of how many workers had indeed been backlisted by such agencies and never found building work again. There are villains on every side it seems...

Well, just as it was looking as though I'd hit a brick wall, Charlie picked up a form.

'Okay,' he grunted. 'If the company is paying the dues, I'll sign the bloody thing to get that berk off our backs. Just for you, Dave. Not for that bastard though.'

Then Danny, the chippie and his mate also agreed to sign. They were going back to Ireland after the contract and couldn't care less. Eventually, the camaraderie of the site won and I had twelve completed forms. We always made a point of having a happy site where the men could joke and take the mickey, and where quarrels and cock-ups were settled quickly and without rancour or recriminations. So I felt that the men had repaid that attitude by helping us out of the awkward situation.

Tucking the forms into my briefcase, I drove back to the office where the battle with the men on site was a mere skirmish to that with our finance department who, like most staff in private contracting, believed that Thatcher was the best thing since sliced bread – especially in emasculating the unions. No way were the company going to pay for union dues.

Luckily, my managing director could see the wood through the trees. On his instructions, with much muttering, they released a cheque for the amount of the twelve yearly subscriptions. This I forwarded to the man's union office with the completed forms and breathed a sigh of relief.

In due course, twelve personal union cards arrived. I took them to site and offered them out during the lunch break. Charlie took his, the others refused outright with ripe suggestions of where I could stick them, and we locked them away in the site-office desk in case the man came around again.

So the cement and concrete and bricks continued to arrive, and the job was finished almost on time. It was sad however, that instead of encouraging men to believe in co-operation and mutual assistance, that Stalinist functionary had probably alienated them for life.

ONE TOO MANY

In over thirty years, I have had only one serious accident on any of my sites. But that was still one too many. And the fact that it happened to Mick, made it all the more painful. Whether it would have been prevented by the vast amount of paperwork generated by successive Health and Safety Acts, CDM regulations, Risk Assessments, Method Statements, Quality Assurance, etc. etc., I am not certain. For it seems that these days, the site agent spends so much of his time filling out paperwork in the site office, that he gets less and less chance to walk the site and see what is actually going on at the sharp end, which is where it all happens – or can go wrong.

This is not to say that assessing risks and preparing method statements for dealing with awkward or dangerous tasks is not essential. Just that a huge paper processing system has been evolved by the pen-pushers, often defeats the object of the exercise – to save life and limb. And with many injuries and several fatal accidents in the Construction Industry each year – there is definitely much to save. In the final analysis though, if the man in charge at the sharp end – the foreman or site manager – doesn't or can't do his job, then all the paperwork in the world won't help. Which is what happened in this very incident.

We were building a new house in the huge rear garden of a suburban mansion. Between this garden and that of the neighbours was a high, one-brick thick, Victorian wall. As the ground on our side was higher than that of next door, and with excavations for a deep drain planned not far from the wall, I instructed the site foreman to prop the wall from the neighbour's side. Which had its problems.

Two retired men lived there and had spent much time and money collecting horticultural Victoriana and appropriate plantings to make it all of a piece. So I spent much time with them explaining why and how we were working next door and ensuring that we would take utmost care and would willingly move any precious stonework ornaments and potted plants away from the wall in time.

'It's OK. I'm making arrangements with next door,' Ken my foreman kept assuring me each time I visited site and found the props – which were specials and had been located with difficulty – still in a neat pile by the garden path, and the precious ornaments still sitting by the wall.

'The digger is coming next Monday,' I warned Derek on my Wednesday site visit. 'Stop everything and start moving all the neighbours' gear away now – and get those props in before the weekend!'

'No problem, he promised. 'We're starting on it today, as soon as you've gone.'

In hindsight, I should have personally checked that it was being done, but then Ken was an old-time foreman - and as it is said: 'You don't keep a dog and then have to bark yourself!' Also, not having received any of the anxious 'phone calls from those neighbours that came from time to time, I took it that everything indeed was being sorted out.

Thursday was spent at another two sites – which had their own problems – and my Friday was as usual spent at head office sorting out time sheets and generally chasing up people and materials to ensure that the following week's programmes had a fighting chance of being achieved. The rear garden wall propping didn't enter my head. After so many reminders and the last warning – and Ken being an experienced man, I took is as done.

And anyway, I'd consoled myself, the digger was still working near the new house, well away from the wall.

Mick was working on the same site. He was an Irish ganger-man, one of those experienced ground-workers without whom the building industry would collapse. If there was an awkward pipe junction at a manhole entry, getting the kerbs in at the correct height and radius, or sorting a difficult junction in the pavings, he would resolve it. Not highly literate, Mick worked as though by intuition, as if he'd been born with an innate sense of direction, symmetry and contouring.

After working on one or other of my sites for about six years, we'd become quite friendly. And with Mick there, I was sure that if Derek didn't move his backside, Mick would make sure he did and would set-up the props and move the neighbours' gear away in time.

But, as Murphy's Laws states: if it can happen, it will.

I tried to phone on Monday morning to see how things were going but for some reason, the phone was dead. The JCB had previously snagged the temporary line once, so I conjectured that it had done it again. But when I drove up on my routine visit that lunchtime, the site was in complete chaos. Men were running in and out of the neighbour's gateway and round to our site hut and back, and the JCB excavator had its bucket down, and was silent.

'Telephone's down,' shouted Jim as I got out the car. The JCB had indeed snagged the temporary overhead line as it moved across the site. But that wasn't the real problem.

'What's up?' I asked, getting out of the car.

'Wall's collapsed,' said Larry, who had just come out of the gateway. 'Caught Mick.'

The digger had apparently progressed more rapidly with the drain trench than had been thought, and Derek, having yet again ignored my warnings and instructions, had suddenly realised that it was nearing the wall. Grabbing Mick and two others, he'd rushed round to set up the props. But he hadn't given notice to the neighbours, so at that that moment one of them had rushed out and demanded that he move the nearby ornaments and pots before propping.

As Derek panicked and ran to sort out the props with two others, Mick began moving the garden objects away from the wall. Unfortunately, with no one directing work on the higher, site side, the JCB driver – who couldn't see over the wall – decided at that moment to stabilise his machine. But as put out his jacks, the pressure on the soil pushed against the wall and immediately, it began to lean. Derek heard the brickwork creaking and shouted to Mick to jump clear.

Mick, who was lifting one of the neighbours' heavy pots dropped it and tried to jump away. But it was too late. And just before I'd driven up, the wall had toppled over and pinned his legs to the ground. Had he not reacted quickly - and had not been caught in soft garden soil, it would have been much worse – or so we thought at the time. Contact with soil though, proved later to be an even greater danger.

These were days before mobiles. I was about to drive to the nearest phone box when by chance Jerry noticed an ambulance picking up a patient from an old people's home opposite. It was not an accident ambulance but luckily they had radio contact and immediately called 999. The men had meanwhile removed the rubble from Mick's legs, and when some fifteen minutes later the accident ambulance arrived and took him away, he seemed too dazed and in shock to even cry out in pain.

Apart from my own horror at what had happened and my agony over Mick, I was furious with Kenk. I don't think I have ever been more angry with anyone in whole my life. After all my instructions, my warnings, his assurances... He couldn't look me in the eyes, and with great difficulty I restrained myself from letting him know exactly what I felt and thought of him. It wasn't the time though. Post mortems would come later. What had happened to Mick – and the certainty that but for his quick reactions, it would have been fatal – will probably haunt Ken for the rest of his life. It certainly does me. But at the time it was Mick that most occupied my mind.

I left them to get the site re-organised again and shot round to the Royal Free Hospital to find out what I could, but was told only that he was undergoing emergency surgery. Then I phoned head office with the bad news and arranged to see the director the following day. There would be some explaining to do.

That same evening I drove to the hospital again and after I explained who I was, they allowed me in to see to him. His legs were swathed in dressings and raised on pillows, his face drawn and pale. He usually had such a healthy, tanned complexion – 'from one of those Spanish seamen shipwrecked in the Armada', he once joked.

He was obviously in much pain but managed to smile and even complained about not being allowed to smoke. He'd been operated upon and the legs could be worse, the doctors had said, but he would get back full use of them, they expected. We even joked about him having to leave the nurses alone. And I drove home feeling just a little less distraught.

Well the next day, not wishing to leave it to Derek alone, I spent the morning on site, organising clearing up the garden, pacifying the neighbours and promising compensation – and arranging to remove the rubble and build the new wall, before returning to the office and to the director to relate what had happened.

In the evening after work, I drove to the hospital and went in to visit him again – only to find the bed empty and made-up! My stomach heaved and I felt quite sick. The nurse saw me standing there, probably looking like a zombie.

'He's been taken to Aldershot,' she said. 'Last night. To a special oxygenating unit.' As I opened my mouth to ask her why, she murmured – as though not wanting others in the ward to hear: 'Gangrene!' And then I remembered the men saying how his legs had been pushed into the wet soil by the weight of the bricks. If they'd transported him by night, I thought, it must have been deadly serious. It was.

I phoned the specialist hospital in Hampshire the very next morning. Yes, he was there but they could give information only to close relatives. Surmising that he must be in a serious condition. I phoned again. Yes, it was me. Yes I am his brother, I lied, desperate to know the worst. And strangely, as I said that, I felt almost as though he was, as if through all those years working and joking on site together, I felt the responsibility of a brother to him in this terrible time. Either way, I learned that his condition had been critical upon arrival but now he was out of danger. The wall hadn't killed him - but the gangrene easily could have.

The following evening after work, I drove down to Hampshire. Mick was sitting up in bed, even smiling. On a bedside chair sat his girlfriend – not very serious he'd joked to me a few weeks earlier when she'd phoned the site while I was there. But *she* was! When he introduced me, she barely nodded and glared at me, as though it was all *my* fault – which I suppose was a reasonable assumption.

We talked. He told how he'd sensed a sweetish smell coming from his dressings and it had taken him a couple of hours to convince the trainee nurse that something was wrong. Luckily, the doctor on night duty was an ex-army man who, when summoned, immediately knew it was gangrene and there followed an excruciatingly painful midnight dash at high speed across London and the Home Counties.

In this special unit, Mick had been enclosed in a sealed cylinder and oxygen pumped in under pressure. The hyper-oxygenated blood slowly pushed the anaerobic gangrene infection down from the legs into the feet and out of his wounds. But it was terribly painful he said.

'Couldn't smoke in there either,' he half-smiled as he related the story. 'I'd have caught fire!'

After two weeks, during which I made several visits, Mick was transferred to another hospital near Slough, undergoing muscle rebuilding and plastic surgery, and rehabilitation. At weekends, I visited him several times and he seemed on the mend mentally as well – often his old joking self. A month or so later, he was discharged and decided to go back and live on his cousin's farm in Ireland. But he was never the same again. And all for the want of a few props at the correct time.

I made out the standard report to the Health & Safety Executive, fully expecting a serious investigation and the prospect of a court inquiry, but to my surprise, apart from the company's internal investigation, there was no sequel.

It took me some effort to face Ken each time on site visits, but we had to finish the contract - and as is often the case, a lot of detail was in his head. The men must have let him know about Mick's condition and he could barely look me in the eye. Eventually the contract was completed and house handed over. Knowing how we felt and expecting the chop, he immediately left the company.

Yes, it was the only one serious incident in my whole career - but it was one too many. And in a well-organised company like the one I was in, unusual. Today, a written risk-assessment and method statement would have been in the foreman's hands in good time, and he would have had to act on it. But again, what if he hadn't? Which boils down to the old problem; no amount of paper work can replace an experienced and conscientious man on site. And I learned from that too – never to rely on promises or reports, but to physically check all the safety precautions instructed. And on subsequent contracts, I always did.

Today, the construction industry is riddled with paper chases: quality-assurance procedures and audit trails all borrowed from manufacturing industry and often unsuited to building sites, most of which are created and dismantled one after the other within the space of a few months or a year. We now have health and safety officers – often made redundant from the decimated coal mines or steelworks and heavy industry, as well as minutely-detailed, computerised, logic-linked programming, created to satisfy planners and quantity surveyors, but often much too involved to be of much use on the average building site.

Then again, most serious accidents in construction take place on unorganised sites run by small builders cutting corners or using young lads for work that only experienced men should be doing. And it is precisely these who require regulating and controlling, rather than the large companies, most of whom already had their own safety procedures and high standards anyway, but who now strive to absorb even more and more of the newly invented paperwork to prove they are 'holier than thou'.

Perhaps the one good thing to come out of new regulations like Construction Design and Management and Health, is the responsibility for safety planning by the client and the designer as well when they are planning a new projects. But either way, I can't help thinking that the site agent having the time to get out of his office and onto the work-face, that will do most to prevent accidents on site.

As for Mick, from time to time one of the Irish

labourers brought me news from his home village, where he was doing odd jobs around the farm with his cousin, his legs in one piece but never as right as they had been. And when I think of him, I still feel sad and bad about that, very bad. It was my only serious accident but like I said: that one was one too many. And I learned from that: where safety is concerned, check personally – and check again, for as Murphy's Law states – if it can happen, it will.

TROUBLE AT T'COUNCIL

The telephone rang with the kind of ring that tells you it is trouble.

'Excuse me,' sounded a polite female voice from the other end, 'I don't wish to make a fuss, because your plumber has done such a fine job replacing our bath – and cleaning up nicely afterwards.' A pause. 'But it is usual for your men to take a bath afterwards as well?' For a moment, I was gobsmacked. Who the heck had done such a stupid thing? Then before I could even respond, she continued, 'and what's more, he came downstairs almost naked – with just a shirt around his waist and asked if I could lend him a towel. Which incidentally, I did.' Pause. 'Is that usual too?'

By her description of the man, I knew it was big Jim.

Profuse apologies and expressions of sympathy defused the situation, and when I put down the phone and relayed the conversation, the office erupted with laughter. It was no joking matter however. I was furious. And I hurried out to my car to pay the lady an urgent visit.

We were engaged on what is known as a Term Maintenance Contract, for a large, sprawling, outer-London borough, and it wasn't without its problems – most of which stemmed from the antagonism of much of the Council's admin staff. And this was just what the gremlins in their offices would use to get at us.

Before making judgement however, after going round to eat humble pie with the lady, I kept any response to myself and waited for big Jim to report back. Having become used to spurious complaints from council tenants and officers, I wanted to hear his side of the story. But the civilised way the woman spoke and acted, already made me fear that there was no other side. Still I wanted to hear Jim's side first – after all, I owed him a big one. Just a few weeks before he'd saved the contract from a truly embarrassing – and potentially costly situation.

We'd been called to a block of flats where many of the residents had a problem of low water pressure. Some of the pipework seemed blocked or furred up, and the job sheet suggested flushing out the system. Well at the suggestion of the Council supervisor, we engaged a pressure jetting company and on the day, they brought this motorised pump alongside and began to connect up to the system. By chance, just before they were about to raise the pressure, big Jim passed by on his way to another job.

'What's that bloody great machine doing there?' he asked our plumber.

'Going to flush the system.'

'With that bloody thing? That'll blow the whole works sky high!'

Immediately they shut off the machine and I got a phone call at the office. Ten minutes later, I was at the flats where Jim took me aside.

'Listen,' he said. 'Who suggested that machine?'

'Someone at the Council,' I said.

His face grew red.

'Thought so,' he said. 'Bastards. Listen, Dave, everyone knows these flats have had water problems for years.' Being a local man, Jim knew all the latest gossip.

'Some cowboy carried out repairs a while ago and cocked it up. Needs a thorough survey and tracing all the main pipe runs. Will cost a bomb so the council don't want to do it.'

'So why did they suggest pressure washing?'

'To drop you in the sh—t, that's what. As soon as that bloody machine would have raised the pressure, a weak joint would blow and probably flood a dozen flats or more! It would be all over the local papers and the company's name would be crap.'

'So it was a deliberate suggestion?' I asked, astonished.

'Listen. You don't know who you're dealing with, Dave. Some of those council blokes up there have been running a nice little show for themselves for years, and your new contract is going to upset all their pretty shenanigans.'

Well, we paid off the machine hire, and they departed. I just couldn't believe it, but I was a relieved man. So indeed I owed him one - but more of Big Jim later.

Our company had won this term contract for two years. It entailed taking over the routine maintenance of local council properties for a term of two years. It is now commonplace in local authorities to do this. At the time though – in the late Eighties – it was part of Mrs. Thatcher's plan to cut the local councils down to size by forcing them to sell off council housing, while at the same time bringing in private contractors to replace their own direct labour building departments.

This contract seemed like a profitable enterprise to

our directors – plus which it was in tune with their political inclinations (though I could never fathom why, since under both Labour or Conservative governments, it made little difference to the successive booms and busts so prevalent in the construction industry).

Our problem with this contract however, was that although the finance department of the Borough welcomed the scheme as a way of saving money, they had to retain much of the administration of the old system in order to inspect properties and give out the work. And the people in this administration, having to dispense with half their operatives and foremen – and a cosy relationship with their pet contractors, feared that they would be next for the chop and thus were less inclined – to put it kindly – see it succeed.

They also managed to convince the borough that it was too risky to privatise everything at once, and so managed to retain half of the maintenance work for themselves under the guise of 'comparing response times and costs'. And this was to become a real thorn in our side.

The contract remuneration was based on the famous – or infamous – Red Book. This was a tome the size of a volume of the Encyclopaedia Britannica, in which every conceivable item of building work is scheduled and given a unit price, e.g. so much for a metre of rafters, or a square metre of brickwork, or so much for replacing a mortice lock, and so on. The scheduled prices were regularly updated in line with the building costs inflation index.

The system had been invented for the Ministry of Defence and served its purpose reasonably well in the building and maintenance of army camps and adjacent housing, and various MOD installations. It was less suited to properties spread over many square miles of an Outer London borough, where one had to travel half an hour through traffic to fix a lock, or glaze a window-pane, and then be paid only the few pounds listed in the schedule.

In order to maximise their savings however, the Borough's sharp-pencilled surveyors had then gone out to competitive tender to several large contractors, asking them to reduce the Book Prices by a percentage, with the lowest one winning. So when we obtained the contract, which was worth about two and half million pounds – quite a sum in the Eighties – it was obvious that our company's 'mark-down' on the schedule prices had left very tight margins. My waters told me that we would be lucky to break even.

To manage this contract, I was asked to create and organise a complete new department – almost like creating a small building company. So in the company car-park, we installed new Portakabins and interviewed and employed secretaries and two supervisors. To find mobile operatives, all with their own transport, we advertised and then interviewed local craftsmen.

When they saw the piecemeal remuneration, many were reluctant at first, but were won over by the prospect of regular work every day, instead of the usual stop and start regime that affects all independent tradesmen. I also made special financial arrangements with many local suppliers, so that the men could pick up materials on demand with new, specially printed order books. And of course there was the mad rush to get all this ready for contract start date, but somehow we managed.

Once the contract commenced, every day one of us would drive to the council admin offices to pick up fresh work sheets, which were logged onto our desktop computers by my new, very no-nonsense, Scots' secretary, who then made a duplicate sheet for each job for our operative. Throughout the day, the men would come in, pick up a bunch of sheets and drive away to pick up materials and carry out the work detailed, while my two supervisors made the rounds to check up and resolve problems. And every day, we would hand in the job sheets of those that had been completed to the council, all the men trying like mad to meet the completion dates, or reporting back anything unusual that was affecting it.

One of our problems was having to deal directly with the tenants. When a large company like ours generally dealt with whole blocks or estates, the estate's holding company or management would deal with the tenants. Now we had to so directly, property by property, tenant by tenant – and not all craftsmen have great diplomatic skills. But so far, we had managed that reasonably well. Which was I so was furious with big Jim.

We found that the council tenants were of two kinds. The majority were perfectly reasonable people but often, having been given the run-around by an inefficient and occasionally skiving, council direct-labour force, were already quite exasperated. Many of their repairs had been bodged or only partly resolved and they were only too glad to co-operate to get the job done. Some, especially the older ones, often offered the men cups of tea.

But there was also a minority of tenants who were a

small band of perpetual complainers. Throughout their tenancy, they had been constantly on the phone to the council – or more often – to their local councillor, complaining. As a result, their homes had every conceivable addition that could be squeezed out of the department – something along the lines of the famous Liverpool family in the T.V. series – just to keep them quiet. Our operatives soon came to know these addresses off by heart and would run bets as to when the next sheet for that property would come in.

Generally, the men did well, but given the size of the area and the number of jobs, there were odd complaints about our work that would wing their way to the council, who then relayed that to my director, often taking up valuable time in explanations. So we needed events like Jim's alleged bath-time escapade like a hole in the head.

I cornered Jim as soon as he stomped into the office with his work sheets. Jim, a big man with a shock of white hair and bristling moustache to match, was an old-timer and prickly to handle, but being a very experienced plumber and a CORGI registered gas-fitter too, he was a valuable member of our team.

'Well,' he explained, as though coming downstairs stark-naked in a strange woman's house was an everyday occurrence, 'the lady didn't seem to mind. And I got in such a mess dragging out the old bath and lead piping – must have been there since Victoria – so I couldn't drive away like that, could I?' Looking quite earnest and self-righteous he leaned forward. 'And I cleaned it all up for her, spotless, bathroom an' hallway an' all.'

The story meanwhile had reached the council, who

lost no time in telephoning the director. So it was a bollocking for me and had to be curtains for Jim. And unfortunately so – because we never found as competent a replacement.

Most of the tradesmen – about twenty of them, were independent sub-contractors. They suffered the council sideswipes and the few irate tenants because it was regular work with a guaranteed daily rate – and a bonus for each job successfully completed. After a few months, we developed a real camaraderie and group spirit in the unit, enlivened by our principal secretary, the mature Scots' lady with her wonderful sense of humour. And as the learning curve flattened out and the men got the hang of the area and the most frequent type of jobs, we began to succeed more and more. In fact, with the help of a specialist Red Book quantity surveyor – and it requires a specialist – against all the gloomy predictions, we even began to show a small profit.

But dark forces beyond our control were at work.

At first sight, the system was fair. Computer-generated work sheets were intended to be randomly apportioned fifty-fifty, between the Council's remaining direct-labour department and ourselves. These work sheets were categorised and given completion times according to the urgency, and then distributed by the council's supervisors, ostensibly randomly. Despite knowing that the council direct-labour administration was antagonistic to the whole idea, we had meanwhile established quite friendly, personal working relationships with quite a few of them. What we did not know though – and what became apparent as the months passed – was that their managers were actively seeking to undermine our contract and make it fail, in order to restore their previous system.

This became apparent after a few months, when it was obvious that we were getting a larger proportion of 'awkward' jobs. Our operatives and supervisors often reported back that they'd been sent to addresses only to be faced with frustrated tenants over jobs that were 'leftovers' from previous attempts, or work that had been bodged. Again and again, we had to divert two or three men to one house to resolve items like long-blocked drains or awkward roof-repairs that had been running sores for years, yet we would only get the scheduled price for the completed job. So after a while, it became obvious that fair play had gone out of the window.

As we had no control of apportioning and distributing the job-sheets at the council offices, we couldn't prove this. But from the frequency with which our operatives came back with the tenant's tales of previous attempts at these same awkward jobs, we guessed what was happening.

'We're just being made the fall guys,' moaned John, one of my supervisors as he drove in one afternoon. 'That manhole was half blocked with solid mortar from when they council men had been there over a year ago.'

Now, many of the council's direct-labour force were conscientious operatives who did a decent job. But with the shortage of competent tradesmen, many 'chancers' had found a comfortable niche in which to slot, and once there, with union backing, were difficult to dislodge. In addition, the council supervisors had also used sub-contractors of varying quality, with whom over the years, a rather too cosy relationship had been built up.

Most of our operatives lived in or around the Borough and had friends among the council employees and workmen. Often they meet them in the pub to chew over the fat and so they regularly came back with 'inside' stories of this property or that. They also picked up rumours of 'goings-on' – of final accounts to favourite sub-contractors allegedly being signed off for more than the jobs were worth, in return for cash back-handers. There were rumours of council officers having built houses out in the sticks, way above what their salaries could have allowed, much of the work allegedly carried out quid-pro-quo by these sub-contractors. In addition, there were tales of materials for council jobs deliberately over-ordered and diverted to these private jobs.

Obviously, nothing could be proved and as stated, it may have been just hearsay, but even allowing for exaggeration, there was undoubtedly fire somewhere amongst the smoke. So our displacing their pet sub-contractors was another reason why some of the council supervisors resented our presence. If our contract succeeded, large contractors like us would take over all the council maintenance work and obviously put paid to all those shenanigans.

Thus we were caught in the middle between the higher echelons and finance department of the Borough who were in favour the contract to reduce costs, and the mid-level officials who wanted to hang onto their perks, and in some cases possibly, their jobs, and would do their best to ensure that the contract would not succeed.

The principle method used to undermine our efforts, was for the council admin officers to make frequent complaints of alleged poor performance, or late completions to our directors and to local councillors.

Each work sheet had a time factor. Some were emergencies, like boilers failing during mid-winter or blocked drains, or storm damage. They were telephoned through and we had to deal with them that same day. Our secretary would write out a temporary job sheet and phone myself or one of my supervisors, and as we drove in, wave it out of her office window. Other jobs had two or three days, or a week, depending on the urgency, and finally there were the larger, 'Void' jobs: making good and decorating properties between tenancies: changing sink-units or boilers, etc. These might take up to a few weeks, and since the council lost rent as long as they were unoccupied, these too had to be finished on time.

Every month, at joint meetings, we had to present a resume of percentage success in meeting these dates and generally, we did well. There were undoubtedly times when out of hundreds of jobs, a few had been completed late for some reason or other – though never the emergencies. At first, we were just asked to improve and it was left at that, and over the months, we did. So towards the end of the first year, with the systems and camaraderie we had established, it was obvious that apart from a few hiccups, our contract was succeeding very well.

As our second year began, we knew that the council was preparing new tenders to be sent out for the following two years. In addition, precisely because of our success, they also wanted the expand expanding the scope of our contract. But now, with that high probability that we might succeed in obtaining one of those contracts, the attitude at council admin offices hardened, and the machinations began.

A few simple failings now brought alarmist phone calls directly to our directors at head office. Luckily, my superiors began to see through this too. Then the monthly review meetings at council offices became more like inquisitions, the small percentage of jobs not completed on time magnified into major disasters. Our requests to see comparisons with their own direct-labour progress sheets were refused, on the grounds that 'it was an internal matter'. With our men's knowledge of what was happening 'out in the field' and their 'inside' contacts, we knew that their completion and complaints' records were very much worse – even though we were given most of the bum jobs.

Despite all that, as time went on, we overcame the steep learning curve and the contract continued to move into profit – and could only get better. From my experience of the monthly meetings at the council offices however, I became convinced that we were in a no-win situation.

The mid-level council officials with whom we worked had the whip-hand both in apportioning the work and in assessing performance. And since they were opposed to the whole idea, they had no wish to be satisfied and it would be a constant struggle. Above all, the constant battle of words, the sniping and the behind-the-back intrigue was wearing. It was destroying any job satisfaction for me as well as demoralising the men and my supervisors. Having built up my unit and seen it succeed; eventually I became fed up with the politicking and back-biting, to which I could see no end.

By chance, at that same time, a contract manager from another department was at a loose end and I was asked to take him into our set-up, despite the fact that we had not yet won the following two-year contract. In that situation, two is a crowd – and in addition he was a relative of one of our directors. The last thing I needed was a clash with sharp elbows. So I looked around and when offered a position in another company, much to the disappointment of our chief surveyor and my director, I handed in my notice, and a month or two later, left.

As for big Jim, I occasionally saw him in his white transit, beetling along the back roads in the Borough to a gas emergency or similar, head thrust forward and white moustache bristling. I just hoped he'd remembered to bring his towel with him this time.

BRINGING DOWN THE ROOF

Apart from fire, nothing does as much damage to a building in so short a time, as water. If it doesn't destroy thousands of pounds worth of newly finished work – for the flood inevitably happens when the job is almost ready for handover – it soaks the fabric of the building so thoroughly – and of course it will be in the winter – that it takes weeks of heating and dehumidifying to dry it out. Either way bang goes the contract programme and up go the costs.

Water leaks have plagued me throughout my whole building career. Similar to my problems with underground water, either through leaking roofs, faulty pipes or overflowing tanks, the wet stuff has so often found a way to cause untold chaos and disruption on one or other of my contracts. As I once mentioned, being a Cancerian, I would have expected my 'water sign' to be more benign. No chance.

Perhaps the most harrowing – and costly – incident, was when we were converting a listed Grade II, old railway hotel into the headquarter offices of a large brewery company in a provincial town. Built in the 1860's, it had once been the grand 'Station Hotel' where, in those pre-motor-car, Victorian days, travellers would have put up overnight waiting for the next day's long distance train – or recovering from the journey before taking the coach and horses home.

After the end of the First World War, with faster trains, car ownership and other means of transport, the hotel was frequented less and less. Soon, only the pub on the ground floor continued to be used, mainly by travellers returning from London. It took another war to give the place a new lease of life.

The older locals regaled us with stories of how, during WW2, the bedrooms of the old hotel had been brought back into use by American servicemen from the nearby air base – the ground floor bar serving as the local pick-up joint. True or false, by the time we took it over in the eighties, everything in the rooms was as it had been left in the Forties, preserved in aspic and covered in dust - as though dozens of Miss Havershams had just been carried out. At the rear was a large cottage-garden that had once provided fresh food for Victorian diners, now completely overgrown and destined to become the new car park

At the first site meeting, the old pub tenants were still there. They kindly offered us a meal but we declined. I was glad we had. When we later went through the kitchens, the grease looked as though it had been there since the Second World War too.

Our first job was to clear all the rooms and corridors back to the bare boards. Most of the contents were cheap 1920's furniture, and every day, truck-loads of soiled mattresses, moth-eaten blankets, bedside cabinets, wardrobes, chairs, etc., went to the local tip. Considering what some aficionados now pay for art-deco furniture these days, we probably threw away a nest-egg, though some of us did salvage the odd relic. I still have a solid-oak, Victorian bosun's chair – they don't make them like that any more. In the lunch hour, one of the chippies removed all the brass knobs and eschuteons for sale to the local antique dealer. But mostly, none of us had the time or energy to suss out a local receiver. Years later, John my surveyor and I lamented the probable loss of a small fortune. It was the one that got away...

The job specification had allotted a Provisional Sum for minimal roof repairs, but apparently no one had actually been up there to survey the situation. The fact that the top floor had been unoccupied for ages however, made it likely that would be much worse. Sure enough, once we had erected a scaffold around the building and climbed up, it looked as though the roof hadn't been repaired since the first war, let alone the second. Many slates had slipped and like most old roofs, not having sarking felt underneath, had allowed rainwater to fall through the top floor and below. The leadwork wasn't in a much better state either, and cracks and slipped sections of gutters were letting in more water.

And as soon as we could gain access to the loft and inspect closer from the inside, we found the inevitable rotten rafters, while those that were still dry competed by having a goodly share of woodworm. Alec, my site agent muttered that the leaks ought to have been sufficient to have drowned the little blighters...

As a result of these closer inspections, during the first month we must have submitted about a hundred TQs (technical-query sheets). The flurry of instructions that came back from the architects soon had the clients wringing their hands at the rising costs, and probably wishing they'd gone for a new building nearby instead of this prestigious, but dilapidated, listed building. Finding experienced craftsmen to fit, 'dolly' into shape and burn-in new leadwork to the pitched roof was going to add to the costs too.

The contract was large enough to warrant my staying on site full time. Alec, short and dumpty but solidly built, was an old-time foreman who had moved up 'from the tools'. There weren't many things about building that he hadn't experienced. During the war he had been a naval man and whenever he need a prompt response, would march sharply into the site office and present the problem as though requesting the range and number of rounds for the for'ard turret. On receipt of the response, either through myself or down the phone from the architect, came a flick his wrist as though about to salute and a smart about turn as he marched out again to sort it out. In a similar manner, he ran the site like a very tight ship – and the men knew it.

My being on site all the time had its advantages in getting prompt responses to the many problems that arose from working in an old, listed building. It also provided an embarrassing and humorous incident for the site staff.

During his school holidays, my young son sometimes liked to come with me on my site visits, and one day he came and stayed with me on this site for a while. He'd been amusing himself with coloured pencils and drawing instruments on my desk when the architect happened to turn up with one of the clients. Alec had just come in with the foreman chippie to report yet another unforeseen snag and the boy had obviously been watching the proceedings and listening all morning. Suddenly, in the midst of everything, he spun round and in a loud, clear voice - that unfortunately everyone heard - asked:

'Dad. Everyone here seems to be doing something. But you don't seem to be doing anything?' Amidst the ribbing that "it takes a wise son... etc.," it took me a while to live that down.

Adjacent to the hotel building was a large stable block around a rectangular, cobbled courtyard, with some twenty stalls that once housed carriages and stabled horses. Some had more recently served as garages. Above them were small rooms, once used by ostlers and stable lads where, needless to say, there was even more wet and dry rot and everywhere, pigeon nests and droppings. So handkerchiefs tied round their noses, the men had to clear that out before any work could begin to replace roofing and floors, and plaster the bare brick walls.

By the end of the contract, they had all been enclosed and fitted out as offices, and so would then be hidden from the public. I couldn't help feeling regret that they weren't just refurbished and left in place. That whole bloc and courtyard would have made an excellent crafts' centre and weekend, 'Covent Garden style' market, and would have brought new life to that end of town.

The ground floor pub was given a complete makeover - styled and decorated to look like it's Victorian original: varnished hardwood bar and furniture, flock-paper wall-coverings, scumbled varnish to replicate a smoke-stained ceiling, and all. From Church Street market, I had also managed to obtain decorative Victorian, frosted-glass panels to fit into the pub windows, which added to the effect.

So despite the huge amount of unforeseen extra work, the project was moving along nicely towards completion. The old garden had been levelled and tarmacked into a large car-park, the roof completely re-felted and slated, and much of the rotten timberwork replaced or treated.

Walls and partitions had been plastered, all the services carcassed and getting their second fix, and final decorations were going ahead. And of course all the upstairs and stable rooms had been computer-wired and fitted out as modern offices for the Brewery Company.

On the first floor, the two largest rooms had been knocked into one to form the new boardroom, all the original cornices and plaster mouldings having been made good. We were lucky to have the services of Ron, an old-timer plasterer who knew to cut out special templates and re-run lengths of Victorian cornice and mouldings that had fallen off over the years. It being a messy trade, his working clothes were always covered in plaster, and when anyone remarked on that, in his broad country accent he would just smile and say: 'Look, to do the job properly, I gotta have a third on the wall, a third on the floor and a third on me clothes!'

So, after nearly a year of challenging work, we were carrying out the final decorations, while an office fit-out company was installing their furniture, etc. On the walls of the new boardroom, an expensive wool-weave wall-covering had already been hung and rolls of new carpet were stored in there ready to be laid. So as I drove home that Friday afternoon, it felt good; in two weeks we would be ready for the final handover to the brewery management.

On Sunday morning, the phone rang. It was Alec. He lived not far from the site and had popped in to pick up some car-park drawings.

'Been one hell of a leak from the tanks,' he said. 'Done a bit of damage.'

Knowing Alec's penchant for understatement, I drove

out immediately to see for myself. On entering the site, my heart sank; water was dripping everywhere.

We had installed new large storage tanks in the roof of the main hotel building. Aware of the dangers, I'd had all the water and heating services pressure tested, so there would be no chance of a surprise flood – or so I thought. In hindsight, knowing of my experiences with water, I should have turned everything off at the mains too. But the plumbers were really experienced men so no one even thought of that, and as Alec locked up on Friday, everything of course had been bone dry.

'Didn't want to panic you,' said Alec, as I pulled in to the car park. 'Had a bit of a flood. Got it all turned off now anyway. But a bit of a mess.' He was always a master of understatement. 'Not a lot we can do more to do 'till Monday anyway,' he muttered. No. There wasn't. Except to walk the site, dodge the drips and assess the damage.

The new boardroom was two floors below the main tanks and by chance – or Fate's malicious design - happened to be directly underneath them. As we climbed the stairs, my heart sank. Although Fred had already closed whatever stopcocks he could find, water was still dripping through the ceilings, and trickling over the banisters and down the walls.

Entering the boardroom room, my worst fears were not only confirmed but surpassed. The old lathe-and-plaster ceiling had been in a reasonably good condition, only requiring some patching up. Now the whole lot had been brought down and lay on the floor, including the two ornate Victorian centrepieces. The cornices to the old dividing wall that Ron had lovingly restored had gone too – together with most of those around the old walls.

All lay in a slurry of old lime plaster – and all over the rolls of new carpet to boot. From the rafters and bare laths remaining, water still dripped onto the soggy mess covering the floor. It was as near a catastrophe as I could ever have imagined - a supreme example of Murphy's Law, i.e. 'if there's the slightest possibility of something happening – it will.' And it had.

I didn't sleep well that night and on Monday morning we held a crisis meeting with the plumbers and my surveyor. It turned out that the mains' ball-valve had become stuck, open. Since when does a new ball-valve stick? That alone though would not have been such a problem, but over that same weekend, only pipe that had not been pressure tested was the one-and-a-half-inch copper overflow pipe from the main tanks. One of the freshly soldered joints had come apart. Whoever pressure tested an overflow? And since when does a soldered joint fail? Talk about Gremlins.

So with the mains live, the tank had filled and overflowed and refilled and overflowed – all weekend. And doesn't it always happen on a weekend – or over a holiday? If Alec hadn't looked in on the Sunday, there probably wouldn't have been a ceiling left in the entire main building. It couldn't have been worse if we had planned it to happen - Sodd's Law in action too.

Well, it now was our problem. There was no way we could claim an extension of time. Nor extra costs. So all the additional programme days that had been built-up from the extra works would now disappear down the pan.

Desperately we mobilised to dry out the building again. It was already a damp October – and doesn't it always happen in the cold, rainy season? We pulled in jet-heaters and de-humidifiers from several plant depots in the area, switched on the central heating and added space heaters. I made out a new programme of works with Alec and in an atmosphere more like a sauna than a building site, week after week, we cleaned up, replaced the ceilings and mouldings, and since the original centrepieces had disintegrated, found new fibrous ones as similar as possible. We also had to redecorate many rooms, re-line some walls and touch up finished paintwork generally. It was soul-destroying, but the men on site pulled out the stops and over the following month gradually it all came together again.

Eventually the contract was completed and we even managed to make the grand opening in time. But it was heartbreaking to have to repeat all that fine craft-work. And all because of a freak combination of a faulty ball valve, a weak soldered joint and of course, it taking place over a weekend. Murphy had again proved infallible.

That was my worst experience, but unfortunately water hadn't finished with me, so it certainly wasn't the last. A few years later, we were a week away from completing another large block of sheltered accommodation flats for a London Borough. The whole had been decorated and new carpet laid along the corridors; the rooms were to be left for the new residents' choice. And again I had a good feeling as I drove home for the weekend.

On the Monday morning, we arrived to find two inches of water over the entire ground floor, soaking the new carpets and creeping up the walls to damage the skirtings and decorations. It took some time to work out what had happened and despite the heating engineer's protestations that everything had been completed and turned off, I knew something was amiss with the piping. And it took me all day to inspect the heating pipe runs and several sheets of drawing paper work out exactly what had happened.

Apparently, on Friday afternoon, probably with his mind already on his weekend ahead, the heating engineer had incorrectly connected up the flow and return pipes to the central heating system. And over that same weekend – always an unmanned weekend of course – instead of the pipe runs remaining dry until final testing the following week, water had flowed into the heating pipes and out of the open, bleeder-valves of the new radiators and flooded everything.

Well, apart from having to replace all the carpet, it took over a month for the floor screed to dry out, delaying the handover for even longer. And again it was a freak occurrence. I mean, since when does an experienced engineer mix up flow and return pipes – and leave all the radiator valves open?

Although those two were the most serious occasions, they were certainly not the only ones. And throughout my entire contracting career, Cancerian or not, I lived in constant fear of that wet stuff.

INTERIOR BY DESIGN

If there is anything likely to strike panic into the heart of a contractor, it is the prospect of an Interior Designer being engaged once the job has started - or even worse - when it is nearing completion. Unfortunately it nearly always is towards the end of the contract, because the client – or more usually the client's wife – who has had some ideas in her head for a while, cannot envisage how they would like the rooms to look from drawings and has to see them almost finished to visualise what they would like the decor to be.

Invariably, he or more usually she, knows a delightful interior-designer in Chelsea who did this wonderful scheme in so and so's house – and of course wants theirs to look even better. As the old joke goes: when asked 'what Period style madam would like?' she replies: 'I want that when my neighbour sees the result, she'll drop dead. Period!'

Working as main contractors on large construction jobs, we generally have minimal direct contact with private client's houses. This is more a specialist market with builders who deal specifically in this work. They generally have a band of old time craftsmen and put in a price that justifies the extra high quality and above all, the patience of Job for the constant attention to the client's whims and changes of mind that such projects require. I've nothing against that. In fact, I only wish that they would take all the private client work. Alas, we occasionally do get lumbered.

Usually it is one of the director's private homes

somewhere in the stockbroker belt, or a plush London pad for one of their offspring or, more often, a special job for an architect or consultant who has brought in a lot of work, and to whom the directors owe a favour. 'My lads will sort it out,' they smile. But often it ends in tears, either for us or the client, or both.

A main contractor's forte is management. We plan and organise the projects, and use familiar sub-contractors who are used to working on large contracts with tight programme times and strict financial constraints. They do an excellent job but are not geared either to appropriately cost nor give personal attention to the whims of a domestic client and the super perfection minutae they are looking for in their own – or a colleague's home.

And there is no point in talking of only one perfect quality. As I once said to an irate lady who complained about her specialist paintwork, 'you don't get Dior couture for a Marks and Sparks price'. If she wanted Dior, she should have asked to be quoted for it. Unfortunately, she didn't see it that way. All work should be to the same quality, she maintained. So back we went to the Dior/M&S argument again. But without much joy...

Large contractors are for large jobs. Private client, personal jobs should be given to those who specialise in them. Yet from time to time, we are called upon to provide a service to which we are not geared. The scene that sticks in my mind is of all the projects' managers at head office suddenly remembering an urgent site meeting and making a bee-line for the doors, whenever the director breezed into the office to look for someone 'to take care of' a domestic contract for one of the bosses, or a consultant.'

Nevertheless, we all get caught now and again. Someone has to do it. 'But why me?' comes the mournful cry. And as if that is not enough, just when the most of the wrinkles have been ironed out and job is being plastered – or even decorated, in bounces the client's wife with a darling man or woman she has discovered: her interior designer.

Now I have nothing against that profession. The results can be seen on umpteen TV programmes where quite pleasant and homely rooms are transformed into something wonderfully exotic – and hopelessly unliveable-in. But if that's what people want, good luck. The problem is that that as stated, the interior designer is inevitably a last minute, walk-on part.

Just when you've broken the back of those rotten timbers, replaced all the old loose lathe and plaster with new partitions and added ornate ceiling covings and moulded skirtings, and when the plumbing is all but finished in the bathroom, suddenly, you are presented with a sheaf of A3 papers showing perspective views of this or that room, together swatches of paint colours and fabrics. It all looks very impressive – but often totally unsuited to the structures and services you've just put in place. The result is that not only we, but also the original project architect are completely fazed.

At one large house in Regents Park, we had almost finished the building works. Having managed to make a human being of the old, irregular lime-plastered walls and uneven floors, we had just commenced decorating, when the lady came in with her interior designer holding a sheaf of beautiful drawings, including designs for linen-stretched, wall-coverings for the bedrooms. Well, just fixing the battens and lining them up on those old, irregular walls would be a nightmare. And that was just the beginning.

In the lounge and dining rooms, ornate lights were supposed to spring from stud partitions, but there was neither cabling nor lighting points, nor noggings to anchor such heavy fittings. In the hall and stairways, walls prepared for papering now required a hard, smooth finish for specialist, glazed paint, dragging and scumbling. In the bathrooms, with the plumbing and electrics already installed, the large standard bath was now to be changed to a hexagonal one plus a Jacuzzi and surrounded by Grecian style pillars.

Remembering an urgent meeting elsewhere, I beat a hasty retreat and left it to my surveyor to acquaint the client with the extra costs – and the arguments that would follow. Yes, we did it, but the programme stretched on and on. In the end the client was satisfied, but the haggling over the final account took almost as long as the contract.

Another memorable time was when we were refurbishing mews cottage in Notting Hill for the manager of an art studio. The large Regency houses in the adjacent streets were once aristocrats', bankers' or rich merchants' town houses, well built and with thick walls and heavy timbers. The mews' cottages at the back however, were intended only to shelter the coach and horses below, and provide meagre lodgings for their coachman above. They were thrown-up as simply and as cheaply as possible.

Today, they are bought by people who could probably afford the main house but already have one in the country, and just want a pied-a-terre in London. Unfortunately, the purchaser is so in love with their 'bijou property' that they prefer to ignore the origin and state of the building - and that to make it as solid and presentable as those main houses, you end up almost demolishing and rebuilding it. And in order to secure the commission, their architect often tends to play down all the dangers lurking – and what it might all cost in the end.

Firstly, the old stock brickwork needs making good and completely re-pointing externally. The woodwork, having been neglected through three or more wars and economic depressions, is full of dry rot or woodworm – or both - so practically all the joinery doors and windows require replacing, and often most of the flooring too – to say nothing of the old lime plaster, most of which has to be hacked off and the walls re-plastered. And of course the old cobbled, stable floor has to be concreted over and screeded or have new joists and floorboards – to say nothing of the old slate roof...

This Notting Hill contract was for just such a mews' cottage; old garage below and a small flat above, during one of those long hot summers As a result of the late-addition designer and her schemes, it ended up as an expensive refurbishment on top of the re-build, incurring lengthy arguments over the many additional costs – though more of that later.

When Pippa, a diminutive, lively brunette breezed into our site in a see-through, gossamer dress, all work practically ceased. We were still in the demolitions phase of the mews' cottage, so Ernie, my foreman gave her a hard hat and conducted her round the site. She was completely unfazed by the lascivious looks from the workforce but I wondered what Ernie accounted the men's idle time to on the daily allocation sheets. Either way, site meetings never had quite the same appeal since.

Throughout the initial phases of the heavy construction work, Pippa, who, it turned out owned a few art galleries, took a personal interest in the work and was overjoyed to see the structure taking shape, making something out of nothing as you might say, since it was almost a rebuild. Indeed, all went well until we'd finished putting in the new first floor and the plumbing and electrics, and were finishing plastering. The architect had made pretty good use of the tight space in the small property and it had all come together nicely.

Then, just as we were about to commence decorating, Pippa suddenly arrived on site with 'My Designer' – a thin, angular woman who had a fabrics' and design shop 'somewhere in Kensington'.

Fearing the worst, we left them alone to wander around the house while I telephoned the office from our ground floor hut, warning my surveyor that we could be on site for an extra month or so. Once bitten…

To the next meeting, Pippa flounced-in in an off-the-shoulder – and not touching much elsewhere – yellow creation, bringing her designer's kitchen and bathroom drawings, of which the salient feature was a sunken bath in the first floor we'd just joisted and boarded. Ernie grew apoplectic and was about to say what he thought when I kicked him under the site table.

'We'll have a look and see if there were any problems,' I told her gently.

'Any problems!' Ernie yelled at me when she'd gone. 'You must be joking!'

Well he made strong tea and the two of us sat down to look more closely at the drawings. Then we calculated the weight of the bath, plus the water, plus her.

'An' her boyfriend,' snapped Ernie. 'Big bugger. I seen 'im!'

Either way, after we would have to cut away the floorboards and joists to fit it in, unless we strengthened the floor structure, as soon as the bath was filled and occupied, the whole lot would probably have ended up on the ground floor.

I phoned the architect. He wasn't that pleased either, but it was her decision, he said. So we had to engage an engineer to make his calculations and ended up with two eight-inch steel beams spanning from wall to wall below. This entailed cutting the already plastered ceiling on the ground floor and later to fit a suspended one.

'Wouldn't give her boyfriend much headroom on the ground floor, that's for sure,' muttered Ernie. Needless to say, the waste pipes and water services had to be completely reconfigured as well as ripping out and re-running the electrics for the new kitchen layout alongside; the designer's lighting scheme to the kitchen ceiling alone would have illuminated Trafalgar Square – how they do love myriad lighting fittings.

Until then, the structural alterations over and above what had been quoted for had already come to a tidy sum. Even without the re-plastering, the designer's alterations would now add a few noughts. Our surveyor advised Pippa of the extra costs, and though it was against my nature, I actually began to feel sorry for the architect. He was as fed up with her designer as we were

– perhaps even more so since he couldn't even claim extra costs even though it had involved him in more inspection work and matching his original design to the new one.

Well, after a few additional months later – and even more frayed nerves – we handed over the job and Pippa was delighted. The crunch came at the last site meeting. My surveyor presented his final account and had had brought it with him. After a sort discussion, she turned to him and waved it in the air.

'Listen. I'm not paying all these extras,' she snapped, 'You should have taken for them.' Then turning to the architect, all innocent, added: 'Why have you agreed all this?' Like many architects, much of his work came through personal recommendation and he didn't want to upset her. He couldn't dispute the figures, yet didn't want to admit them and, as often, dithered.

Slapping the table, Pippa then turned to me.

'You are the experts,' she snapped, the sweet, demure personna suddenly transformed to that of a harridan, 'you must have anticipated all that re-furbishing.' In vain I carefully explained the effects of her designer's late changes, the considerable additional work involved and the additional time on site, etc., etc.

'Maybe,' she snapped. 'But it wasn't that disruptive?"

Ernie blew up.

'The bath? Not disruptive?' Even my kick couldn't silence him this time, as he rattled off a string of alterations in the services, the steel beams, re-plastering etc. etc. Pippa listened, completely unimpressed as the architect explained her obligations under the contract. When he'd finished, she turned to my surveyor.

'Well I'm just not accepting all those costs,' she snapped, standing up and pulling on her jacket. The flimsy creations had gone and a cool autumn breeze was blowing in through the window. 'You can add two thousand and that's my final offer,' she said and flounced out, calling back as she went out. 'Sue me if you like. I've got three other court cases on the go already.' Which, we found out, she did have.

What do they say about the most beautiful snakes having the most deadly bite? She'd probably short-changed her interior designer too.

There are lots of stories from people who paid good money for sub-standard building work and many of these have substance. There is much less publicity about small professional builders driven into bankruptcy by unscrupulous clients who were perfectly able to, but had no intention of paying the justified costs right from the outset. And using the interior designer sometimes seemed just another ploy in their game.

Well we pursued the rest of our money through the architect by quoting the contract, but in the end had to write off a loss. We were part of a large company and could stand the odd knock. It would have driven a small builder to the wall.

Either way the introduction of an interior designer to the contract will always flag up warnings – on programme and on costs – and but above all, on site nerves. Thankfully, during my entire career, I didn't have that many with which to cope.

LIFT UP

In any new, high-rise building project, the first thing you notice during the construction is the central concrete-core going up – the spine of the structure, which encloses the lift shaft and often, the escape staircase. That is the easy way of putting in a lift. Much more complicated is fitting a new lift and its shaft, into an old building.

Adding new floor or a penthouse suite to an old building usually demands a new lift - or an extension to the existing one. And with so much modernisation or change of use, a new lift was essential in converting the many institutional buildings in London that dated from the Thirties or before. So in the Eighties and Nineties, there was 'a lot of it about'.

Similar to a new building, installing a lift involves also requires a completely new, fireproof lift shaft. This ensures that if there is a fire on one floor, people can still get out – or if there is a fire travelling up the lift shaft between floors, it will be contained.

This particular project arose with the expansion of university education - and the desire to recruit more overseas students for greater profitability. And in this particular, renowned London college, the student body had almost doubled over the years. The result was massive congestion, especially at the beginning and end of the day in the ground floor entrance lobby, as a milling crowd waited for the single lift to come down from one of the eight floors. To resolve this situation, we were contracted to install a new lift – in a new shaft, on the opposite side of the lobby to the existing one – and all while the college was in occupation.

Installing the actual lift car and winding mechanism is, for the contractor, the easy part. It is the job of real specialists who would work like troglodytes inside the shaft hidden from everyone, just emerging for lunch or to go home. The more awkward part is forming a new lift shaft in an occupied building.

In this contract, it entailed breaking out large, square openings, one above the other, through each of the eight reinforced-concrete floors, all within lecture rooms and offices, as well as through the roof. At the same time we had to keep the building watertight and free of dust and debris, and of course operating as a college throughout.

In these days of multiple paperwork: method statements, risk assessments, company safety-officers, quality assurance, etc. etc., it is interesting to look back at a complicated and hazardous job like that in the Eighties, where the only instruction about methodology or anything else apart from the specification and drawings, was a nine or ten-line statement on the engineers' plan drawing, giving the proposed sequence of work. Yet the job went safely and – 'as sweet as a nut'- as we say.

Our main work was similar in principle to framing a new staircase in a domestic house, inserting new floor joists to trim round the intended opening, before cutting the stairwell in the wooden floor. The difference here though, was the floors were of reinforced concrete – and to frame the new lift-shaft opening and preserve the stability of the rest of each floor, we had to install heavy steel beams from wall-to-wall, under these concrete floors. And of course, with all this work being carried out while the college was in occupation and working, we had to make sure it remained watertight and dust free, and reduce noise disturbance as far as possible.

Prior to starting work, on the roof we erected a 'shed' of scaffold tubing and corrugated sheeting over our proposed new shaft opening. Then we had to erect dust-tight hoardings in the lecture rooms, but also across the entrance lobby and on each floor, which unfortunately created even more congestion during the contract.

Once this had been done, our first task was to divert all adjacent electrical, IT and plumbing services. Then prior to cutting the lift-shaft openings, we had to raise and install the long, heavy steel beams, and install them under each floor. The beams were far too long and heavy to be manhandled up the existing staircase, so after making small aperture in each floor, we set up an 'Elephante', an electric motorised cable hoist on the roof slab and slowly hoisted the beams one by one. With four beams to each floor, there were 32 in all - many of them twenty feet long and each weighing around half-a-ton, it was a delicate operation. So on each floor, as the long steel beam came up, one of our men guided it through the hole -'like threading a bloody great needle,' one of them joked.

From then on, on each floor the procedure was the same. First to cut holes in the adjacent brick walls to take concrete padstones, which would support the beam ends. Then two main steel beams were levelled and set onto the stones, and two similar 'trimming' beams were raised bolted onto those main beams with cleats, steel angle-pieces, all to create the heavy, four-sided frame. Once these steelwork frames had been levelled and fixed on each floor, we could begin to break out the concrete floors for the shaft.

Unfortunately many of these walls abutted classrooms and lecturers' offices, and although the college was officially on holiday in late July when we commenced work, the many staff still marking exam papers or working on research projects, didn't take too kindly to coming in one morning and finding a beam-end hanging over their desk, or plaster dislodged and messing up their papers. The college admin, it seemed, hadn't always thought of informing them what was about to happen.

We had programmed most of this heavy work to take place during the long, hot summer recess, but since the college was still occupied and many staff were still working, most of this heavy and noisy work had to be carried out at night. Early each morning, I would come to meet with Gary, the Site Agent - burly, fair curly haired and great sense of humour - which didn't comer amiss on such a project. Usually I founding him and most of the night shift stretched out amongst the tables on the college terrace-café, drinking subsidised Coca Cola in the morning sunshine and chatting up students who were still around.

Over a coffee, the two of us would sum up the previous night's progress, discuss any problems that had arisen and plan the night ahead. I would take his order for materials or messages to the sub-contractors and we'd walk the site - and then I would throw them all out to go home and get some sleep. Sometimes I felt that if I hadn't turned up, he and the men would have been there all day, enjoying the ambience, the sunshine, the coke – and of course the students.

All through that hot summer, floor by floor, the steel beams were manhandled, winched up, erected and bolted together. Tightening the connecting bolts by torque-wrench to the engineer's specification in the confined space was not simple either. Finally, when all the steel frames were in and set on their padstones to support the floors, we could erect access scaffold and cut the actual openings for the new shaft.

Inserting the steel beams had taken up most of the holiday recess, so to speed up progress and keep to our programme, we now had a day shift as well whose main job behind those hoardings, was to cut out the actual openings on each floor. By now though, the college term had commenced, so to avoid excessive noise and vibration, we brought in demolition specialists using special hydraulic crunchers. These machines, looking like mechanical dinosaurs, had tungsten-steel teeth that crunched and nibbled away the concrete floors silently, bit by bit during the day. At night, when we could use the more noisy Kango hammers, we finished off the internal corners and smoothed out any rough edges.

Although steel is a very strong element, in a fire it is weakened and distorts, which could lead to a complete structural collapse. So as in all steelwork constructions, the beams have to be fireproofed, in our case, by encasing them in concrete. For this we had to form plywood troughs around each beam - no easy matter in the confined spaces of the shaft. Then, during the day we poured in the concrete around the beams to several floors at a time using a concrete-pump lorry from below.

This machine and concrete lorries created unavoidable chaos in the approach road to the college from Kingsway – which had to be arranged with the council and the police. And with the concrete-pump hose snaking through the lobby and up the shaft openings, we tried to schedule the actual pours for the early hours before the students came in nine – not always successfully managing to finish in time.

At last, after several weeks, all these apertures in the eight floors were complete. At last we could begin to build the blockwork walls and form the actual shaft itself, working from the ground floor up to the roof, and forming new lift-door openings on each of the eight floor lobbies as we went.

For the college staff, the first real relief came in the Spring term. After we had plastered the walls facing the lecture and study rooms, and offices, we could remove the safety screens and return them to their occupants. The next stage was plastering the public lobbies walls on each floor. Only then could we remove all those hoardings and reduce the congestion on the landings, leaving just lockable temporary doors across the lift openings – securely locked when we left each day - lest some inebriated students found a shortest way down from the top floor at night.

The one thing a lift shaft has to be, is absolutely perpendicular. If it is out of plumb even by a small amount, given the height the lift car travels, it would snag and not pass through. To ensure this, we fixed four heavy steel angles at each corner of the shaft to support the lift apparatus, and to guarantee absolute verticality, set up a laser beam apparatus on the top floor. With the help of its red beam, the angle steels were meticulously plumbed vertical and aligned before bolting them to the walls.

Then, praying that it would not rain that day, we removed the temporary hut on the roof and planned for a lightweight fibreglass cabin – like the ones you see in industrial estates' gateways - to be delivered and hoisted by crane, a hundred and twenty feet into the air and set down on the roof over the opening and bolted down. This cabin would serve to house the electric lift-hoisting machinery at the top of the shaft. Despite being scheduled for a less busy Saturday morning, the delivery low-loader and the huge crane required for such a height and weight created yet more traffic chaos in the Aldwych, to which having been forewarned, the police were very helpful.

As for similar manoeuvres on any of my sites, we always met with the local authority highways people and the police many weeks before to discuss the situation, and to fix a convenient date - and I must state here that they were always extremely helpful.

So when you curse the traffic diversions caused by one of these monsters in a busy town road, spare a thought for the project manager who had negotiated with - and paid - the local authority to close the road, the police to divert traffic, and to re-assure the crane hire company that all this has been done - and most critically, ensure that the load to be lifted is delivered at the same time, because if not, the whole, costly procedure and chaos has to be repeated a few weeks later.

With the work to building the new shaft now complete, we fixed the 'lifting-beam' at the top of the shaft. This has to be pre-tested to ensure that it could carry the full weight of the lift car in the event of repairs or emergency works. Instead of suspending several ton weights to test it, a specialist company attached cables, securely anchored to firm concrete below, and applied a tension equivalent to the weight required, then stamped its SWL – safe working load - on the beam. And so, with the lift shaft and beam completed, at last it was time for he lift engineers could come in to install the lift.

It seems that whatever their company name, the lift installers are invariably a small family group of two or three who have been a lifetime in the game, man and boy, some of the men well past retirement age. In this field, it is experience that counts. Slowly and methodically, they hoist the lift-motor up the shaft and into the roof housing, then string up long lengths of cables while at the same time, building the actual lift-car inside the shaft. Their work time is incorporated in the contract and often takes up half of the programme period.

Working at their own speed – and with the responsibility to ensure that a dozen people are safely hoisted a hundred feet or more every few minutes without a mishap, they continue methodically day after day, take no chances, and will not be hurried. To deal with a very unlikely failure crash event, we concreted a special hydraulic piston into the basement floor of the lift pit which, if all else fails, is activated by an accidental car free-fall and springs up to cushion the landing.

Once the physical lift installation was complete, floor by floor, other specialists came to install all the electric control points and services, with their miles of electric cabling, and set up the lift-doors and push buttons and indicators on each landing.

Eventually, the day came when all had been tested

and we could remove the last hoarding across the lift doors. The Principal and college staff who had all been suffering the noise and dust, trooped into the lobbies over nearly a year, entered the lift car and pressed the buttons, and lo and behold, without a hitch, up it went. Student congestion problem solved.

We packed up our last bits and pieces of plant and surplus materials and melted away. No one enquired about who did it or how. We managed as usual and just completed the job.

A few weeks later I returned to check on a few items. Standing in the ground floor lobby and watching both lifts going up and down, no one would ever know that it hadn't been like that ever since the college was founded.

THE CLERK OF WORKS

The Clerk of Works stomped into the site hut while I was on a visit; check shirt, neat collar and tie and thick, white naval socks turned over the tops of his rubber boots. He nodded to Bert, the foreman.

'Just had a look at your brickwork,' he said meaningfully, and laid a closely written sheet of paper on the desk. 'Generally okay - but I'm not very happy with the gable ends on block four. Need to sort it out.' Nodded to me, and went out again.

'Ah well,' moaned Bert, the foreman, glancing the pages with a painful expression on his lined face after the man had gone out. 'Must have had a row with his wife.'

Bert was an old-timer, shiny bald-head and lined face. Not many things about the industry he hadn't met, so I was surprised.

I glanced through the list. Uneven joints, chipped corners of bricks, perpends out of line, mortar in the cavities. The site was a new council housing estate, occupying several gangs of brickies. But I also knew that on that particular block we had employed a new bricklaying gang the week before.

'Is the work really that bad?' I asked

'Not really. Mostly it's pretty good. Come and see.'

'How often do you get these?' I asked as we walked towards the scaffold.

'Once a week, regular,' grunted Bert. 'Usually on a Monday.' He shrugged, 'After a miserable weekend and a row with his wife I suppose.'

Ernie was the Clerk of Works, an almost mediaeval title that perhaps denoted an attitude. They are not a common feature now, but in the days of massive local authorities' and government works, they were found on most building sites. The Clerk of Works (COW) was appointed by the client to ensure that the building would be built as designed, and in accordance with all the British Standards and Codes of Practice that the contractor had signed up to.

Isn't that the job of the project architect, you might ask? Well it is, except that many young architects haven't the necessary practical experience to pick out the faults in workmanship – and the more experienced ones are often into higher things. So the COW was the man on site who looked after the client's interests and ensured that the work was carried out exactly to specification.

The Clerk of Works usually came from a trades' background, often having been apprenticed as a carpenter/joiner and trained in the old school to the exact niceties of good craftsmanship. He would know his building fabric details from A to Z.

For example, if the specification called for all joinery timber to be 'knot, prime and stop, undercoat and 2 full coats of gloss', his job was to ensure that the contractor did just that, as stated and was to be aid for.

In most cases, some kind of rapport was established between the site management and the COW, which was just as well, for the man's word was law and it was useless to dispute it. All you could do was to accept that some of the criticisms were relevant, try to soft-talk those that were nit-picks and somehow reach a modus vivendi. After all, he was being paid to ensure that the contract was being carried out to specification – and with much of the work parcelled out to sub-contractors on a price, there was always the danger of their cutting corners.

When problems did arise on site, they were often more of a psychological nature or from a clash of personalities. And as the whole industry became more professional, despite more qualified and competent site agents and management, the COW was determined to preserve his status and position. Some would do this by endless criticism and rubbishing of work on site – and like an absolute monarch, he had no fear of contradiction - as in the old biblical expression 'the servant who would be king.' Whatever he said or wrote would be backed up by the client and the architect, since he was their appointee and none of them felt technically equal to him.

Thus a length of wall could be condemned and had to be pulled down, or extra nailing or screwing of timbers had to be carried merely on his say-so, all because without remedying what the COW considered 'defects', the architect would not agree the work and no payments would be made. That's how it was.

To be fair, with few directly employed craftsmen, and the work now being carried out by sub-contractors on a price, there was at times a tendency to cut corners and for some men to try to 'get away with' whatever they could. The problem was that there was no arbiter and there was no appeal. The COW was judge and jury.

Perfection might be attained in a trade exam or on prestige jobs where cost was no option, but at times there appeared no recognition at all of the real world. And many a contract – or even a contractor – had gone to the wall as a result. We often joked that the more obstreperous and difficult COWs would have done well under Stalin. Luckily these were few and far between.

Ernie actually wasn't that bad. He would sometime sit in our site office with his lunch of fish and chips from the local Chippy and chat. Many of his ilk refused this kind of social contact – as though it would compromise them.

Under the contract, we, the contractor had to provide the COW with a site office, complete with drawing table and chest, desk, chairs, lamps, heater – you name it. And whilst the site agent often had a bare undecorated hut with wooden floorboards, the COW had to have floor covering and painted walls. Knowing the power he had and also acknowledging his building experience, our site agents usually treated him with respect and despite the odd confrontation, tried to forge an amicable relationship.

The COW was of course just another human being and when there was a personality clash between him and the site agent – many of the 'defects' would be magnified as ammunition in the power struggle, with the heavy guns obviously on the COWs side.

Occasionally, this led to a ridiculous situation – as in one case with which I had to deal; that of Mac, the inebriated Clerk of Works.

Mac liked his tipple. We didn't know that of course but perhaps should have guessed, from the ruddy complexion and the smell of spirits in his breath whenever he came on site. He was the Local Authority Clerk of Works on a large, school upgrade project in Central London. At first he and our site agent seemed to get on fine – no complaints just the odd note or two, and things were jogging along nicely.

We had however, recently established a no-drinking policy on all our sites, which meant that the traditional lunchtime binge was out. In an industry that had until then marched on its beer bellies, it wasn't all plain sailing. And on this project our site agent, Ricky, was one who liked his tipple too. But he was keeping to the rules – or so I thought – until more than a few times I couldn't contact him by telephone around lunchtime.

So I programmed my next site visit for just after lunch. Sure enough, around two o'clock in bowled foreman Ricky with Mac, the COW, both obviously having had more than a bevvy or two. I waited until Mac had gone, then confronted Ricky.

'You know company policy,' I said gently. 'How come?'

Ricky's face already flushed from the wet lunch hour, grew even ruddier.

'I've got to go,' he groaned. 'Mac always calls in at lunchtimes. Needs a drinking partner. And one day when I didn't want to go, he got right stroppy and started walking round the site, pulling this and that to pieces even though he'd ticked them off the day before.'

So we made a plan of action. I would time my site visits for lunchtimes a few days a week so that Ricky would be 'busy' when Mac popped his head in. And it appeared to work. Except that about two weeks later, we began to get contractual letters from the council architect about the quality of work on site, site safety and so on - all apparently as reported by their COW. It was baffling. Until then, everything had been fine and we'd been no change of personnel or sub-contractors that could have affected the work.

Ricky was upset by the reports too when I called round to discuss them.

'It's Mac,' he said. 'He's annoyed with me because I've stopped going out lunchtime with him. Says he doesn't like drinking on his own.' He held up a bunch of site notes. 'And he's started slipping in these defect reports each day. Pain in the neck.'

No nothing had changed, except that we'd annoyed the COW. But what could we do. Complain to his superiors at the council? He would deny it and with his word against ours, they would back him to the hilt. And on site Ricky's situation would become even worse.

Well the letters kept arriving at head office and Ricky and I were at our wits' end. I had explained the situation to our director, but there seemed no way out of the impasse. Fortunately I found one.

I deliberately arranged to meet the Borough architect on site just after lunch. And as we sat in the site office looking at some drawings, in walked Mac with Ricky – completely tanked up and almost unintelligible. After the usual greetings, the architect said he wanted a word with Mac, ostensibly about some brickwork. They went out together, and didn't come back.

The following week, we heard that the man was transferred to another department in the borough. Ricky joked that if he hadn't been, we might still been on site to this day!

Which is what indeed almost happened with another COW on a large council housing project in Southall.

This Clerk of Works had once been a site foreman in our own company - but unfortunately not a very competent one. After demonstrating his incompetence on a couple of contracts, he had eventually been dismissed. He was one of those who should have remained a tradesman and probably would have done well at it, but having had the requisite paper qualifications and the gift of the gab, he had somehow managed to obtain a post as COW at the local council. Three years later, by chance he was appointed COW on this particular project.

My site agent, Chris, happened to know him from 'the old days', and warned me that there was bound to be trouble. And from the moment the man first appeared on site, indeed there was.

'I know your lot,' the COW said to Chris. 'And there won't be any short cuts. I'll see to that.' And he kept to his word, day after day condemning work and once almost heaving over a length of cavity brickwork.

'Rubbish,' he'd snorted. 'Bloody improver could do better!'

Chris had his work cut out preventing the brickies from laying him out there and then, and at the next site meeting the architect quietly agreed that the man had overreached his function. Which only made it worse on site. Informally, I spoke to the council's building manager and the project architect, but although they sympathised with us, there was no way they could not back him. This was in the days of strong unions in the council building department. Removing him might have led to an all-out strike.

On site, the atmosphere was sullen. Sub contractors didn't turn up, site meetings recorded increasing delays and financially the contract was well into the red.

'I'll make sure the company regrets ever firing me,' the COW snapped at Chris one day. 'You'll never get off this job as long as I'm here.' And by repeatedly condemning good work, he meant it.

It was a contract we still might never have completed, except that God must have been on our side. It was a nasty winter and the man caught a bad case of flu with complications, and was off for over a month. Chris reckoned that Dick, the brickie had been sticking pins into the man's effigy. During that time however, we managed to persuade the council building department to use his absence by putting someone else on the job – after all it had been delaying the completion of their new housing estate too.

The new COW was more professional and fortunately stayed there until the end. By that time the contract had gone well into the red. But at least we managed to eventually finish and hand it over.

But to go back to our beginning, Ernie wasn't either vindictive or bent. Probably like most COWs, just a punctilious and a conscientious craftsman. From time to time, his neatly written notes would appear on Bert's desk. Bert would swear and cast doubts on Ernie's parentage, but it was nothing disastrous – and sometimes justified. And on completion of the contract, successfully, we invited Ernie into the hut and presented him a new pair of thick, white, knee-length naval socks.

IT'S THE CONTRACT, STUPID!

There is an apocryphal story of a Chinese merchant and a British Importer, meeting in Singapore many years ago over a sale of palm oil. After the endless cups of green tea and sweetmeats, they agree on the sale of fifty barrels of oil at an agreed price, whereupon the Importer takes out a sheaf of closely written sheets.

'Right,' he says, 'now we can both sign the contract,'.

The merchant looks surprised and waves the papers away.

'Look,' he says, 'I want to sell the oil. You wish to buy the oil. We have agreed a price. This satisfies both our interests. So who needs a contract?'

Alas, it is no longer the way. Today, raising a new building on a green-field site or converting an old warehouse into a state of the art facility, should similarly be a work of common aims and combined efforts. Instead, again and again, we come away – even from a successfully concluded enterprise for all concerned – with a bitter taste from the continual running fights between the Builder and the client's agents: his Architect and his Quantity Surveyor. And primarily because of 'The Contract'.

Admittedly, building projects are a little more complicated than buying barrels of vegetable oil, but the same philosophy could apply. The client wants a building, the builder wants to build it and they agree a price. Unfortunately, it is nothing like that. Instead right from the start, most contracts set up an adversarial process with the client's architect and the builder being two completely separate – and often warring - parties.

As a result, the project often starts in an atmosphere of mutual suspicion between the builder and the architect. The architect – who is *de facto* the client's agent despite officially being 'independent'- suspects that the builder will use every variation and delay to excuse faults and delays, and increase profits. The builder suspects that the drawings, specification and Bills of Quantity do not accurately reflect the work and he will be lumbered with resolving problems and filling in the gaps which, through no fault of his own create delays and increase his costs,

As each is bound by the clauses of the contract, they will try to utilise these clauses to ensure that they will not be used against them to apportion blame for any delays or extra costs. Each is determined that it should not be *their* side at fault and it is the rare large contract that doesn't end up with some kind of confrontation.

These conflicts stem from several fictions that are perpetuated by those who advise clients – whether private, corporate or public. The first is that the most economical price is obtained by competitive tendering. It may seem to be the cheapest by asking contractors to compete and so trim the costs, but it certainly does not give the best value for the money expended. Apart from periods of boom – during which no sensible client should build anyway owing to high costs – it sets contractor against contractor scraping away at his prices to be the lowest. And despite the 'health warning' on the tender that the lowest price may not be the one accepted, in ninety-nine cases it is.

This forces the successful contractor to use every clause in the contract to claw back money and reach the correct price that his more careful rivals had bid – and what the true cost really should be. It seems to elude those concerned, that a 'Negotiated Contract' whereby the contractor's price, though rightly questioned and scrutinised by the client and then mutually agreed, rarely exceeds what would have been the competitive sum. It also leads to much more harmonious relations and therefore a smoother, building operation. Yet in the building world, negotiated contracts are a small minority.

The second fiction is that the architect is deemed to be an independent party and can adjudicate fairly throughout the contract. It is obvious that as a paid servant of the client – even with his supposed 'professional integrity'- he cannot be independent. The common joke amongst contractors is whether anyone had met an architect who ever admitted a mistake? It is never *his* mistake – always the workmen, the materials, management etc., etc. Because if he admits a mistake, he will have to admit it to the client who employs him. And as the architect is beholden to the client for payment and for possible future work, even with the best of intentions, out the window goes any impartiality.

Even worse was that in once commonly used forms of building contract, the architect was set up to be the manager of the whole project. Now an architect's forte is his ability to design, to see things in three-dimensions, to utilise space aesthetically and to its best advantage. He rarely has, nor need have, the management ability or the drive and energy required to progress a construction project to its conclusion. That is the contractor's forte. But through the adversarial nature of the contract and tendering process, that energy and skill is often diverted into repeated confrontations over late instructions, programme delays, apportioning blame for poor workmanship and contract clause interpretations.

As a result of the competitive tendering process and common forms of contract – and there are now innumerable variations – the courts are full of building contract disputes that often drag on for months and even years, the only winners being the legal eagles, some of whom specialise in building litigation, and who's practices grow larger by the year.

Some surveyors and architects I knew spent much of their time as 'expert witness', earning considerably more in fees from court cases than from their practices. Many of the larger contractors have one court case or another going on the whole time. What a way to run an industry!

Not that contractors don't have some sympathy for architects in the existing system of things. It seems that just as the client is advised to take on the cheapest contractor, so it seems that he sometimes takes on the cheapest architect. And having been taken on, he (and now more and more often, she), has to limit the amount of time they can afford to devote to the project, and so to the quantity and quality of the drawings provided. A few property developer's contracts I have worked on, seem also to have used half-trained surveyors or cub-architects - probably at cut-price fees.

An extreme example I met, was on a half-million-pound conversion of a block of flats, in the Nineties. At first, we couldn't understand why all the site meetings had to be at half-past seven in the morning and end by nine. It turned out that the project was being designed and managed by a local authority architect who was doing an early morning 'fly-job'. Again, it may have been be the cheapest – but was it value for money?

Responses to queries took ages to come through, so the project lagged behind programme and disgruntled sub-contractors, unable to keep going and make it pay, produced less than first-class work. Just as the householder looks for the cheapest builder and lands up with a cowboy, so the penny-pinching client ends up with poor quality finishes and delays.

Another fiction is that having a hard-nosed principal quantity surveyor (PQS) keeps the client's costs down. The actual result is that there are constant confrontations over monthly valuations and holding back of monies for no apparent reason, which leaves the contractor's surveyor to find ways and means and his own tricks to make up the unjustified shortfalls. It also affects the atmosphere and willingness on site to work together to resolve problems.

The competitive tendering process inevitably forces the main contractor to fight his own corner. Most main contractors now employ sub-contractors, and when the main contract sum has been cut back to the bone, in order to make it pay, this penny pinching is transferred down to them. In lean times, sub-contractors desperate for work often take it on at poor rates just to ensure some kind of cash-flow, and again this can only lead to cutting corners on the work.

Often, even when valuations have been agreed, the main contractor resorts to making delayed payments to sub-contractors to increase their profits, resulting in yet more disharmony, all of which again affects relations on site and the quality of the work. One only has to read the newspaper reports of large contractors leaving sub-contractors deep in debt when they go into liquidation. As a result, there have been legal attempts to ensure that the sub-contractor is paid when the main contractor has been paid, and many large contractors do abide by this, but many do not.

So, as stated, when there is fairness, and a reasonable, negotiated contract price has been agreed, both the client's and the contractor's quantity surveyors can establish a professional working relationship. There may still be bones of contention as work proceeds, but they are dealt with in a workmanlike manner and with give and take, amicably resolved.

And this 'professional' business does get up our nose a bit. We main contractors regard ourselves as professionals. But somehow, an RIBA or an RICS surveyor is deemed to have some higher standing and 'morality' than the contractor despite his man too being a CIOB professional. It certainly didn't stop Poulson or other 'professionals' when they went their own crooked way.

To me, a professional is one who puts his profession first, that is doing a good job to the best of his ability. And we consider ourselves as true professionals, whether members of a Chartered Institute – which many of us are – or not. It's the professional attitude to the project that matters, not the framed certificate on the office wall.

There is of course a way to avoid these damaging and costly contract conflicts. One, as mentioned previously, is to use negotiated contracts between clients and contractors who have built up a trust over the years. A well-known nationwide retailer and one large contractor have in fact been doing this for decades, but very few others seem to have learned the lessons. The second way is to bring more and more projects into the Design and Build framework of contract. To return to the ways in which the cathedrals were built – designer and constructor working with one mind and in harmony.

In this method, the client gives an outline specification of what he wants to a joint team of architects and contractors. Using the architect's talent for design and the contractor's experience of materials and methods of working, the client is presented with a project to suit his needs. It will also be one that can be built in a safe and efficient manner, to an agreed price and on which, cordial working relationships will ensure the best result. Gone will be the tendency to blame delays and extra costs on lack of information from the architect, who will in turn look for the contractors failings – real or alleged – to progress the works diligently. Everyone is part of one team and all share the responsibility for the project finishing on time and to the required standard.

It is true that some architects feel that having the contractor raise practicalities throughout the design process, hampers their exploration of novel ideas and possibilities. Possibly, in a few, very high-profile, one-off projects, it may be advantageous to give the imagination free reign. But for ninety-five percent of construction work, there are only advantages to the design and build method. So why is it the poor relation in today's contracting world?

Most probably it is from inertia and entrenched positions. Competitive tendering and the standard forms of building contract are familiar animals and even with the disadvantages outlined above, everyone knows how to handle them.

Unfortunately, in many cases, even in design and build contracts, the architect is 'novated' by the client and the design is almost complete, so that the architect has become the client's agent de-facto by the time the contractor has to take him on board. This can defeat the objective of giving the design-and-build team the independence to come up with the best solution – both design and construction wise.

Until these or similar modes of contract are more commonplace, there will always be the contractor's suspicion that the architect, as the client's agent, is there to reduce costs and blame the contractor for all unforeseen events on site. And there will always be the architect's suspicion that the contractor is using every clause in the contract to claim additional costs for fictitious delays and lack of information. And only the legal-eagles will profit.

The Construction Industry offers so many opportunities for job satisfaction and personal initiative. It is a pity that this is so often drowned in unnecessary confrontation and bitterness.

And it's all because of the contract, stupid.

Construction Project Managers. We are the ones who tie all the ends – and beginnings - together.

Once we are handed a project, it is our baby. For it succeed, to materialise on the ground from the paperwork as designed, on time and within budget, is down to us. It can be made more difficult with duff sub-contractors, poor design, awkward architect, impatient client, bad estimating or extreme weather - but in the end, as it is said, the buck stops with us.

Construction Project Managers originate is different ways; some have started on the tools, became foremen and site mangers then felt able to move on up into project management. Others studied technical subjects at college and feel they want to get into management at the sharp end. Still others studied management at university and realise that construction offers the challenge that appeals. And in whichever building company I worked, there was usually a mixture of all of these.

Often we occupy a complete floor at head office, which is handy, since as well as listening to each others moans and groans - which inevitably there are, we can share problems and sometimes help one another with advice of this or that sub-contract or plant, or new materials – or even loan subbies to help out in a crisis if our own contracts allow it. And of course there was always the opportunity to take the mickey or commiserate, and share the inevitable humorous incidents. Despite working alongside one another, we are all so involved and busy with our own contracts, that we have little time for 'management elbows' and backbiting, that can bedevil other industries.

Each new project begins the same way. Once the company has won the contract, the director or senior manager decides who will manage it, and if me, for better or for worse, it becomes my baby. The first job is to gather all the relevant material: Bills of Quantities, Specification, Drawings, etc., etc., and look for a quiet spot and spend time to go through them all – not always easy in a busy office, and sometimes in the peace and quiet of my car. Then I drive out and visit the site, which is often an eye opener, often having to report back site 'nasties' which hadn't been taken into account – especially items like difficult access, congested sites, possible awkward neighbours or long-term, nearby road-works.

On very large contracts, the company Planner would have made out the construction programme, and I would sit down and go through it with him. On most of my contracts however, I was given a start and completion date, and after consulting with our estimator who had based his quotation on the period required, I would make my own draft programme. Then after consulting with the principal sub-contractors to get their ideas, I could finalise the programme – usually in the form of a bar chart.

In recent years, many sophisticated programming modules have been downloaded onto our computers with 'logic-linking' the various activities etc., but I confess that if I wasn't handed one from our planner, I often preferred to rely on my own experience and that of the main sub-contractors to draw up the contract programme. Then I would sit down with the project surveyor - usually a just a desk or two away – and go over it with him – usually a him – only in the new century did more and more women begin to make their appearance on the construction industry floor.

If the architect hasn't nominated any sub-contractors as part of the contract – usually specialists – the surveyor and I would draw up a list and he would suss them out, obtain their quotations, and eventually decide which one, then draw-up a sub-contract with them. Often he would choose the cheapest quote, but if I'd had had a bad experience with any of them in the past, we had to sort it out. Above all, we had to work as a team and generally did – amicably. Of course, different companies had different procedures, but is how we usually worked.

The Project Management floor has its own culture – with its own humour – often enlivened with tales of how a pet domestic project is going at home, and one weekend, I wrote this:

On Monday morning, as usual Barry strolls into the office and thumps his briefcase on the desk. Hanging his jacket on the back of the chair, he heads straight for the vending machine to make a strong cup of coffee, the first of several he might need to get through the day.

'How's it going?' asks Alan.

'Got the damn RSJ in this weekend at last,' sighs Barry.

'Come to work for a rest, eh?'

''Bout it,' says Barry, wearily taking out the sheaf of mail that has accumulated in his tray.

Over the last few months, Barry had been building an extension to his dining room in the rear garden at home. That is after he'd finished putting in a new bathroom, a downstairs second-loo and shower. Which was after knocking through a wall to make a larger kitchen as well rigging up a kids' play area in the loft the year before.

'Clerk of Works happy with the job?' chivvies John as he passes on his way to the laser printer.

'She'll have to be,' murmurs Barry.

Of course, he could have got in a builder to do the works. But that would have added another debt on top of his mortgage – which is high enough already. And with two young children and his wife not yet back at work, those repayments are already onerous.

In many households, such upgrading plans would have just had to wait. But when you have a builder in the family – no matter whether you are a surveyor, estimator, planner or project manager – it's seen differently. And of course we all have full time, stressful managerial jobs to start with.

Some men seem to enjoy the permanent weekend building projects at home, and as far as this domestic work is concerned, there are two types amongst us.

The first is the frustrated entrepreneur. He would just love to be the boss of a medium sized building firm, but of course lacks the necessary capital to get it going. He really should have had his eyes on the daughter of a millionaire from the start, so that daddy could have provided the necessaries.

Having missed that opportunity, he starts by buying a small house, works hard to improve it, then sells it at a profit and moves up to buy a larger one. All of which generally pleases his other half as well. After a few years however, having knocked this house about too and enlarged/improved it, and sold it for twice the purchase sum, they move into a much larger place in a smarter area. And after a while, the process begins all over again.

Either way, their house is inevitably a permanent building site and every few years, upgraded and enlarged, off they upwardly mobile go to a larger house and a more 'desirable' location. If his other half has similar ambitions, all well and good – but to avoid marital strife they should have sussed this out beforehand.

The other type is the 'hobbyist', the DIY fanatic who, having building knowledge and ability, goes far beyond the DIY stage into major works: taking up whole floors, inserting steel beams and making loft conversions etc., so that one part of the house – or often several parts – are like permanent miniature building sites.

Here too, the other half can feel herself blessed – or in despair – for if the wife wants some stability to bring up the family that has arrived by now and is happy with what they have, the husband's perennial DIY building works can make her life a misery. If she was any judge of character, she should have held back at the altar, for married to this type, her life will become that of a modern gypsy, constantly living in a building site then moving on – divorce surely never far from her mind.

And, I suppose, there are the two types of wives – those who prefer their other halves to be with the family and live a quiet life – and those who feeling that they have had the luck to marry a builder, proceed to expect him to be just that in his spare time as well as having a regular job. And like I said, if the two ambitions coincide, despite the house being permanent building site, harmony reigns all round. At least for a while.

For others, their wife is the motivator.

'Is that why they marry them?' I sometimes wonder. She inevitably wants a new kitchen, the bathroom remodelled or a new patio or garden-room? And when there is a builder in the house, there seems to be no excuse not to do it. So whether he is the first type or the second, there is hardly a man in the office who, at one time or another, is not converting, adding, putting in new central heating or demolishing and rebuilding his house.

If however, hubby has had enough at work all week – and often overtime as well on awkward contracts – but she still expects the new through lounge and new kitchen/bathroom/whatever, toute-suite – it can create tense marital situations. Someone could probably obtain a PhD on this subject, starting with amassing divorce statistics from these activities.

The other side to the permanent 'home-improvements works' man is, as always, the limited budget. As a result, such staff are always on the look-out for materials remaining on site at the end of each contract. Inevitably, there are lengths of timber, conduit, plastic trimmings, un-returnable ironmongery and sanitary fittings, odd facing bricks, etc., left over on site. 'Just recycling,' we joke, 'that's what it is.' As a result, their garages at home – or an odd room if there isn't a garage – are stuffed full of various building materials that 'may come in handy one day'.

Eventually these materials take over all available free space and when the other half can't get her car into the garage, or needs the room for a new child's bedroom, a general clear out is instructed. By Sodd's Law - or similar - invariably the very day or week following his taking the stuff down to the dump, something that has just been thrown out is just what would have been perfect for an urgent job in the house.

As well as materials, these projects of course require mechanical plant. Hiring plant is expensive, so Kango hammers, heavy drills, grinders, ladders, etc. already on site, disappear over the weekends into the car boot and as the weeks pass, the surveyor's or project manager's smart company car begins to look more and more like a builder's van.

Time and again, after a weekend break-in on site, before complaints are made to the police, the first people to ask about missing tools are the projects' manager, site agent or surveyor themselves.

'Sure you ain't got it at home?' is the inevitable question when something goes missing.

Still, every occupation has its 'fringe benefits'. Those are the builders'. And with the constant 'improvement' works on their houses, a vital consideration.

As for Barry, by the time the family is able to take that long postponed break in Majorca or the Canaries, he finds that his shorts need a tighter belt and his hair, freed from plaster dust, suddenly takes on its natural hue. Until the next project.

So that is the lot of the project manager – a hectic life at work – and sometimes an equally hectic weekend at home. But boring - it never is.

Time to down tools...

Also by David Merron

Goodbye East End - An Evacuee's Story

Collectively Yours - Kibbutz

About David Merron

The writer was born and grew up in London. After finishing Grammar School, he lived and worked abroad for a while. On returning home, he became a Projects' Manager in the construction industry and qualified as a Member of the Chartered Institute of Building. He also has a Master's degree from UCL.

He has been writing for many years and is a published author. He lives in London and is married with three children.

13352433R00155

Printed in Great Britain
by Amazon